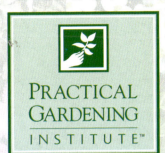

8 Months of Color
for USDA hardiness zones 4, 5, 6 & 7

Janet Macunovich

www.PracticalGardeningInstitute.com
The online community for people who love to garden!

PRACTICAL GARDENING INSTITUTE™ SERIES

8 Months of Color for USDA hardiness zones 4,5,6 & 7

Writer: Janet Macunovich

Editor: Mary Lore

Contributing Editors: Lisa Cassidy, Steven Nikkila and Premier Communications Group: Doug Konen and Kate Pultz

Photographer: Steven Nikkila

Cover and Layout Design: Lisa Cassidy
Manager, Book Production: Lisa Cassidy
Indexer: Lisa Cassidy

Proofreaders: Steven Nikkila, Jaclyn Rooksberry and Margaret Thele

Practical Gardening Institute

President, Chief Executive Officer:
Mary Lore

Vice President, Chief Learning Officer:
Janet Macunovich

Vice President, Member Services:
Karin Andresen

Manager, Communications:
Lisa Cassidy

Special Thanks to: Patty Alba, Karin Andresen, Nicholas Stavropoulos, and to the readers of Janet's *Growing Concerns*™ column who so generously shared their gardening experiences and bloom time observations.

Photographs Copyright © 2005, Steven Nikkila

Copyright © 2005, Janet Macunovich and Practical Gardening Institute.
All rights reserved. No part of this book may be reproduced, distributed, or displayed without written permission from Janet Macunovich and Practical Gardening Institute; nor may any part of this book be stored in a retrieval system, or transmitted in any form or by any means - electronic, mechanical, photocopying, recording or other - without written permission from Janet Macunovich and Practical Gardening Institute.

The information provided in this book is true and complete to the best of our knowledge. All recommendations are made without warranty or guarantee of any kind whatsoever on the part of Janet Macunovich and Practical Gardening Institute. Janet Macunovich and Practical Gardening Institute disclaim any liability in connection with the use of this information. For further information, please contact the Practical Gardening Institute, 29429 Six Mile Road, Livonia, Michigan 48152.

Neither Janet Macunovich nor the Practical Gardening Institute assume any responsibility for any damages, injuries suffered or losses incurred as a result of the information and recommendations published in this book. You use this book and the information and recommendations herein entirely at your own risk. Always read and observe all of the safety precautions provided by any tool or equipment manufacturer and always follow all accepted, reasonable or applicable safety precautions.

The names Practical Gardening Institute™ and The Gardener's Personal Trainer™ are valuable trademarks and/or servicemarks owned and used by Practical Gardening Institute. Growing Concerns™ is a valuable trademark owned and used by Practical Gardening Institute and Janet Macunovich. These trademarks and servicemarks distinguish the goods and services of Practical Gardening Institute and Janet Macunovich and may not be used by any other person or entity without the express written permission of Practical Gardening Institute and Janet Macunovich.

Some text Copyright © 1995, Perennial Favorites.

Printed in the United States by Color House Graphics, Inc.

Published by the Practical Gardening Institute 2005
ISBN 0-9774969-0-2

We are professional gardeners, educators and authors. We are dedicated to bringing you the most innovative, practical instructional materials and information so that you can gain the skill and confidence necessary to design and grow fabulous gardens. If you would like to purchase other gardening books and products or to become a member of the Practical Gardening Institute, the online community for people who love to garden, visit us at **www.practicalgardeninginstitute.com**.

PLANT HARDINESS ZONE MAP

This book contains information that applies to Zones 4, 5, 6 and 7 as shown here on the USDA Plant Hardiness Zone Map for North America, provided by the U.S. National Arboretum, USDA-ARS.

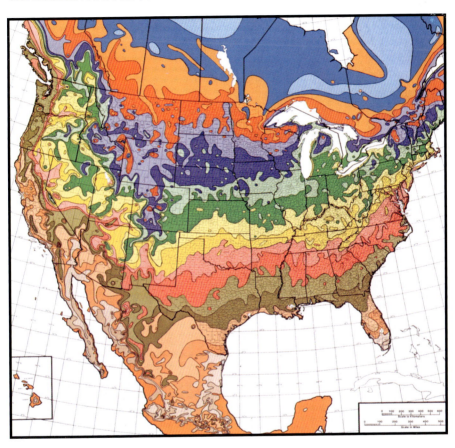

Average Annual Minimum Temperature

Temperature (°C)	Zone	Temperature (°F)	Temperature (°C)	Zone	Temperature (°F)
below -50	1	-45.6 & below	-17.8 to -20.5	6b	0 to -5
-45 to -50	2a	-42.8 to -45.5	-15.0 to -17.7	7a	5 to 0
-40 to -45	2b	-40.0 to -42.7	-12.3 to -15.0	7b	10 to 5
-35 to -40	3a	-37.3 to -40.0	-9.5 to -12.2	8a	15 to 10
-30 to -35	3b	-34.5 to -37.2	-6.7 to -9.4	8b	20 to 15
-25 to -30	4a	-31.7 to -34.4	-3.9 to -6.6	9a	25 to 20
-20 to -25	4b	-28.9 to -31.6	-1.2 to -3.8	9b	30 to 25
-15 to -20	5a	-26.2 to -28.8	1.6 to -1.1	10a	35 to 30
-10 to -15	5b	-23.4 to -26.1	4.4 to 1.7	10b	40 to 35
-5 to -10	6a	-20.6 to -23.3	4.5 & above	11	40 & above

MORE FROM JANET

Books

All About Successful Perennial Gardening
A quick and practical guidebook for preparing a perennial bed, choosing plants, planting and tending the garden. This isn't a boring manual but a straight-talking, fully illustrated reference complete with a full color perennial encyclopedia and dozens of charts and helpful tip lists. When you need help getting started with perennials or improving what you already have, this is your guide to a garden showplace.

Caring for Perennials
You can have a spectacular perennial garden with a lot less work than you think. In "Caring for Perennials," you'll follow everything that happens in a perennial garden from earliest spring to late fall. It's chock full of practical how-to advice organized by time of year, topic and plant species including a chart of what to do when for over 80 perennials. It's also an irresistible read that will give you a whole new perspective on the life of a garden. You'll love this straightforward how-to for getting the most out of perennials.

Designing Your Gardens and Landscapes
Now in its second edition, this book is not just for the new gardener but a valuable reference for anyone looking to design like a master. Part guidebook, part workbook, you'll love the easy step-by-step recipe for creating a beautiful garden or an entire landscape. There'll be no more "Where should I start?" or "What do I do next?" Use this book to design from scratch or infuse new design ideas or classic principles.

8 Months of Color for USDA hardiness zones 4, 5, 6 & 7
Carefully researched and thoroughly documented, this is an amazing compilation of plants by height and week of peak color specifically for USDA hardiness zones 4, 5, 6 and 7. The calendar in the first section of the book offers a visually unique way to make your selection fun and simple. All the plants are described in detail, with tips on how to grow them most successfully. The companion poster graphically presents the information in quick-read style against a calendar—perfect for planning your designs.

All these books, including 8 Months of Color, are available at www.PracticalGardeningInstitute.com in the Gardeners' Market.

Weekly Advice Column

Growing Concerns™ Weekly E-Column
For down-to-earth, practical advice you can't find anywhere else, subscribe to Janet's popular weekly *Growing Concerns™*, offered exclusively to members of the Practical Gardening Institute. You can also access twelve years' of previous columns, by season and by key word, so you can get relevant information when you need it most.

To become a member, visit **www.PracticalGardeningInstitute.com**

ABOUT THE AUTHOR

Janet Macunovich is well known and much loved in the gardening community. An **author** and **educator** in landscape and garden design, Janet has been **designing, planting** and **maintaining gardens and landscapes for more than twenty years**.

Janet's horticulture background includes extensive coursework at botanical gardens, colleges and universities. She is an **Advanced Master Gardener** and has **authored nine books** currently available throughout the U.S., Canada and England. Janet has developed and presented seminars and workshops to prestigious garden and landscape organizations throughout the country. She hosted a weekly radio program in Michigan and for twelve years published a weekly newspaper column in the *Detroit News*. This column is now offered exclusively to members of the Practical Gardening Institute at **www.PracticalGardeningInstitute.com**.

Janet, also known as **The Gardener's Personal Trainer**™, is recognized for her down-to-earth style and her ability to take the mystery out of gardening and design. In 1996 she co-founded the **Michigan School of Gardening** to provide high-quality, practical training in all areas of gardening and design. In 2004 she co-founded the **Practical Gardening Institute** to make practical training and timely advice available to gardeners everywhere.

ABOUT THE INSTITUTE

Someone once said that gardens, like people, can be temperamental. But ask anyone with a backyard bench in a lush garden or a vase bursting with just-cut blooms, and gardening can seem like life's most pleasurable pursuit. It's just that gardening can also seem a little mysterious at times. Well, finding answers you need is a lot easier now. The Practical Gardening Institute has opened a whole new world of possibilities online. **We are dedicated to bringing you the most innovative, practical instructional materials and information so that you can gain the skill and confidence necessary to design and grow fabulous gardens.** Institute members can learn new gardening skills and techniques, participate in forums, attend events and discover answers to vexing questions. We also publish a signature series of books written by our own experts that present information in dynamic new ways.

As an outgrowth of the **Michigan School of Gardening**—*the first and only school of its type in the country*—the **Practical Gardening Institute** has an amazing foundation and resources. We are professional gardeners, educators and authors. More importantly, the Institute is comprised of down-to-earth, knowledgeable and passionate people who love to garden. It's a place for both rookies and advanced gardeners to find a wealth of information. In everything we do, our goal is to enable our members to create wonderful, welcoming gardens. The results? You'll see them all around you—in front yards and back, in community gardens and even on windowsills!

Becoming a member is easy—just log on to our web site. As a member, you'll receive "Growing Concerns," the weekly advice column written by author and gardening expert Janet Macunovich, exclusively for members. It's packed with helpful advice. You'll also be given access to the searchable library of past "Growing Concerns" columns—it's a deep well of knowledge for those who love to garden. Then there's the Gardeners' Forum—a fantastic resource that includes advice, encouragement and suggestions from our team of professional gardeners and industry experts, as well as from your fellow members. Of course, you'll also get discount pricing on all your purchases from the Gardeners' Market. Members also get special pricing on upcoming seminars and events, in addition to special offers from sponsors and friends of the Practical Gardening Institute.

Come grow with us at **www.PracticalGardeningInstitute.com** — the online community for people who love to garden!

TABLE OF CONTENTS

HOW TO USE THIS BOOK 2

SECTION ONE - BLOOM CALENDAR

March 4
April 5
May 6
June 8
July 10
August 12
September 13
October 14

SECTION TWO - PLANT DESCRIPTIONS 15

INDEX 46

8 Months of Color

HOW TO USE THIS BOOK

Hello Friends and Gardeners,

If you're like me, you want as much color as possible in your garden, every day of the growing season. You also recognize that this is quite a challenge, given that peak bloom for each perennial, shrub, vine or tree lasts just two to four weeks. It's the gardener who combines plants to peak together and in succession who will enjoy the longest show. I've found the biggest obstacle in this quest is to locate references that include bulbs, perennials and woody plants, and also pin down peak bloom periods. So many books and catalogs cover just one category of plant and are vague about bloom time. They describe a plant as blossoming in "mid-spring," or claim it "flowers all summer." Without more specific information, we designers can't be sure when "mid-spring" arrives in our garden or even if "mid-spring" is the same in one reference as another.

We at the Practical Gardening Institute recognize and embrace the realities of gardening. We developed this book to let you plan for, and around, peak bloom.

8 Months of Color was thoroughly researched. From 1985 to 1995 I tracked the peak bloom of perennials, shrubs and trees that I used in designing gardens. This greatly simplified the design process: I would list plants I might include in a new design, find those species on my calendar, note color gaps or clashes, then proceed with or revise my design.

I shared the calendar with my students. The word spread and people started asking for a copy of that rough calendar. In 1995 I invited readers of my weekly Growing Concerns™ column to add their observations to my record. In return I sent contributors the compiled calendar. Gardeners in Zones 5 and 6 participated the first year. Intrigued by the differences in bloom times between zones, I expanded the study to include Zones 4 and 7. Over the years since, I've added more species.

This book gives you an easy way to choose plants by week of peak bloom, color and height. The Calendar in section one presents plants in a unique way to make your choices visually fun and amazingly simple. In section two, plants from the Calendar are described in detail. You can locate plants by their peak bloom period or through the Index where both their scientific and common names are listed.

Two Ways to Use This Book

This book and poster are easy to use. You can leaf through the Calendar to look for plants that will fill color gaps in your garden. You can read more about the plants listed on the Calendar in section two, called Plant Descriptions. Plants are listed in this section within their half-month of bloom, and then in alphabetical order by the names as they appear on the calendar.

Alternatively, you can look in the Index for plants you already grow. You'll find them listed under both their common name and scientific name. You can follow the page numbers shown in the Index to see what species bloom at the same time, just before and just after your plant.

The Calendar lists plants that come into peak bloom during a particular month, and indicates whether the peak bloom usually occurs during the first, second, third or fourth week of the month. Although bloom times may vary with weather conditions by a week or two from year to year, the sequence of blooms will generally remain the same.

In compiling the Calendar, I learned that even though species bloom up to twelve days earlier in warmer zones than in colder zones, that difference is restricted to April and May. Then, plants in colder zones rush to catch up. (More plants bloom in June than any other month.) After June, the hardiness zone makes no difference in peak bloom time. From July through mid-October the continental garden is in concert.

Some plants may not bloom as long where the summer is warmer. In fall, some plants in warmer zones bloom for longer periods or develop a second flush of blooms because frost comes later. Yet such plants' *peak bloom* still coincides with their counterparts in cooler gardens.

Where there are spring differences, plants are listed in the average, Zone 5 calendar position. Gardeners in Zones 6 and 7 may find that some plants listed here as early April bloomers may produce a late March show instead. A Zone 4 gardener may decide to change the early April heading on a page to late April. Yet the design system will still work for you, as it does for me when I design for my clients across those four zones. The sequences and combinations described throughout this book still hold true.

Plant names followed by an asterisk tend to have a peak bloom period that is longer than average. If grown in ideal conditions, such plants are likely to remain at peak bloom for five or more weeks.

On the Calendar, plants are separated by height and category as follows:
Short 1 to 12 inches
Medium 1 to 3 feet
Tall over 3 feet
Vines, shrubs and trees

The color of the letter in each plant's name indicates the flower or fall leaf color of that plant. For example columbine is available in pink, yellow, blue and rose. White flowering plants are listed in black type.

I hope you enjoy looking at and using 8 *Months of Color* as much as I have enjoyed putting it together for you.

Happy Gardening,

Janet

The Gardener's Personal Trainer™

MARCH

	PERENNIALS & BULBS			VINES, SHRUBS
Short	Medium	Tall		& TREES

Week 1 (1st - 7th)

Week 2 (8th - 14th)

snow crocus snowdrops winter aconite			spring witchhazel

Week 3 (15th - 21st)

Iris reticula Lenten rose skunk cabbage Dutch crocus			silver and sugar maples cornelian cherry* contorted hazel

Week 4 (22nd - end)

viola/pansy* squill			

8 Months of Color

APRIL

PERENNIALS & BULBS			VINES, SHRUBS & TREES
Short	Medium	Tall	
Week 1 (1st - 7th)			
Adonis *Draba Haynaldii*			
Week 2 (8th - 14th)			
puschkinia wild violets* tarda tulip *Tulipa turkestanica*	early daffodils		red maple
Week 3 (15th - 21st)			
spring beauty Dutch hyacinth hepatica marsh marigold *Pulmonaria saccharata**	Greigii tulips Kaufmaniana tulips		star magnolia Japanese andromeda forsythia (dandelion!)
Week 4 (22nd - end)			
Dutchman's breeches *Aubrieta deltoidea* pasque flower *Primula x polyantha**			ornamental cherry dwarf fothergilla

8 Months of Color

MAY

	PERENNIALS & BULBS		VINES, SHRUBS & TREES
Short	Medium	Tall	

Week 1 (1st - 7th)

trout lily toothwort myrtle euphorbia myrtle (Vinca) grape hyacinth Anemone blanda	leopardsbane merry bells summer snowflake daffodils, late varieties Brunnera macrophylla*		saucer magnolia callery pear serviceberry apricot quince

Week 2 (8th - 14th)

woodland phlox ajuga Bergenia species creeping phlox foamflower perennial alyssum sweet woodruff perennial candytuft Epimedium species	celandine poppy Anemone sylvestris large-flowered comfrey cushion spurge* mid-season tulip large-flowered trillium rock cress	money plant bleeding heart fringed bleeding heart	PJM rhododendron Koreanspice viburnum clove currant redbud

8 Months of Color

MAY (CON'T)

PERENNIALS & BULBS			VINES, SHRUBS & TREES
Short	**Medium**	**Tall**	

Week 3 (15th - 21st)

geum sea pinks* mouse-ear forget-me-not vernal sweet pea *Veronica prostrata*	columbine catmint* Virginia bluebells Alpine aster	dame's rocket*	flowering dogwood Burkwood viburnum crabapple redtwig dogwood slender deutzia bridal wreath spirea Amer. cranberry viburnum common lilac

Week 4 (22nd - end)

creeping soapwort dwarf bearded iris *Dianthus species* lily of the valley star of Bethlehem *Potentilla*, herbaceous spp.	late tulip red field poppy *Camassia cusickii* mountain bluet perennial geranium* Canada anemone* oxeye daisy* culinary sage *Trollius* white baneberry heucherella	gas plant swamp buttercup* *Euphorbia griffithii* willow amsonia *Verbascum phoenicium*	Carolina silverbell Siberian pea shrub/tree *Calycanthus floridus* Vanhoutte spirea red horsechestnut Amur honeysuckle Dutchman's pipe vine nannyberry viburnum alpine currant Europ. cranberry viburnum snowball viburnum Exbury azalea horsechestnut Sargent crabapple

8 Months of Color

JUNE

PERENNIALS & BULBS			VINES, SHRUBS & TREES
Short	Medium	Tall	

Week 1 (1st - 7th)

strawberry	iris, bearded types	Siberian iris	Japanese kerria
snow-in-summer	red baneberry	lupine	Amur maple
blue-eyed grass	coral bells	Iceland poppy	Europ. mountain ash
blue fescue	Crambe maritima	ornamental rhubarb	autumn olive
creeping baby's breath	Solomon's seal	blue oat grass	honey locust
pussy's toes	Dianthus species*	oriental poppy	cotoneaster species
prairie smoke	perennial gladiola	angelica	golden chain tree
creeping forget-me-not*	Bowles golden grass	Centaurea dealbata	alternate-leaf dogwood
Allium species	Pologonum bistorta	giant allium	wisteria
	Allium species	yellow flag iris	cut-leaf stephanandra
	clustered bellflower	false indigo	American elderberry
	dropwort	foxtail lily	tree lilac
	Nectaroscordum siculum		dwarf lilac Miss Kim
			Korean lilac
			hawthorn species
			doublefile viburnum
			arrowwood viburnum

Week 2 (8th - 14th)

cheddar pinks	sweet William	Rodgersia species*	weigela
Irish moss	lemon lily	peony	Potentilla, shrubby spp.*
common tyme	painted daisy	foxglove (biennial)	kousa dogwood*
yellow hawkweed	Jacob's ladder	Crambe cordifolia	mock orange
mouse ear coreopsis	pea vetch	Valeriana officinalis	black locust
self-heal	milfoil yarrow*	meadow rue	Robinia x ambigua
lady's mantle*	Salvia superba*		beauty bush
Phlox ovata	Salvia species		climbing hydrangea*
early ladies' tresses	spiderwort*		large-flowered clematis*
Sedum, short early spp.			sweet bay magnolia*
			ninebark*
			firethorn
			tulip poplar
			common privet

8 Months of Color

JUNE (CON'T)

PERENNIALS & BULBS			VINES, SHRUBS & TREES
Short	**Medium**	**Tall**	
Week 3 (15th - 21st)			
birdsfoot trefoil* blue fringed bleeding heart *Corydalis lutea** Anacyclus depressus	*Hosta* spp., early blooming crown vetch swordleaf inula *Penstemon* species blue flax *Achillea x taygetea** lanceleaf coreposis *Iris pallida* Astrantia species* Oenethera speciosa *Scabiosa* 'butterfly blue'* common harebell *Salvia verticillata*	goatsbeard Carolina lupine early Lilium species *Verbascum* Cotswold hybrids	Washington hawthorn graystream dogwood northern catalpa *Clematis recta* dwarf spirea* Heckrott honeysuckle* *Rosa multiflora*
Week 4 (22nd - end)			
Jasione perennis lemon thyme Missouri primrose Carpathian harebell* *Potentilla astrosanguinea* Polygonum affine* Geranium dalmaticum Oenethera caespitosa	pincushion flower* *Gaillardia* species* *Knautia macedonica** early/repeating* daylily wood lily scarlet campion* feverfew* *Hosta* spp., mid-season biennial blackeye Susan *Veronica* species* Japanese iris lamb's ear threadleaf coreopsis early astilbe hybrids	delphinium fireweed perennial sweet pea *Digitalis* species yellow yarrow* golden Marguerite* *Lysimachia punctata* bull thistle	linden *Clematis viticella* vine euonymus winterberry bottlebrush buckeye Virginia sweetspire

8 Months of Color

JULY

PERENNIALS & BULBS			VINES, SHRUBS & TREES
Short	Medium	Tall	
Week 1 (1st - 7th)			
Coreopsis rosea Astilbe simplicifolia* dwarf goatsbeard	butterfly weed lavender lady bells calamint blue linaria Cupid's dart Sanguisorba obtusa sundrops primrose Lysimachia ephemerum madonna lily	Bupthalmum salicifolium sea holly Lilium species mid-season daylily Heliopsis scabra* Lysimachia ciliata Maltese cross baby's breath Jupiter's beard Phlomis russeliana	snowball hydrangea* smoke tree* buttonbush Stewartia pseudocamellia oakleaf hydrangea* Ural false spirea* chestnut
Week 2 (8th - 14th)			
Hypericum calycinum	Heuchera x brizoides California hyacinth Serbian bellflower Sidalcea species Shasta daisy Chinese lantern early astilbe hybrids	pale purple coneflower* hollyhock mallow* rocket ligularia bee balm red hot poker ribbon grass yucca queen of the meadow bear's breeches	Hypericum shrubby spp.

8 Months of Color

JULY (CON'T)

	PERENNIALS & BULBS		VINES, SHRUBS & TREES
Short	Medium	Tall	
Week 3 (15th - 21st)			
Stokes aster	Hosta spp., mid-season German statice* balloon flower Veronica longifolia * sea lavender Allium senescens	gooseneck hoary vervain hollyhock late season daylily queen of the prarie Phlox maculata* Rudbeckia maxima Liatris spicata blue globe thistle purple coneflower* crocosmia blackberry lily Cimicifuga racemosa	golden rain tree summersweet clethra blue/pink hydrangea trumpet vine*
Week 4 (22nd - end)			
edelweiss	bouncing Bet Moonbeam coreopsis* Goldsturm rudbeckia* Achillea 'The Pearl' Lobelia siphilitica*	Phlox paniculata* x Pardancanda norrisii Joe Pye weed culver's root Astilbe taquetii Physostegia, white late season Lilium Russian sage* swamp milkweed Anemone x robustissima	

8 Months of Color

AUGUST

	PERENNIALS & BULBS			VINES, SHRUBS
Short	Medium		Tall	& TREES
Week 1 (1st - 7th)				
Allium senes. glaucum	white flowered hosta patrinia* dwarf & early goldenrod Clara Curtis mum		prairie dock *Ratibida laciniata* northern sea oats cardinal flower* *Monarda fistulosa* Liatris aspera hardy hibiscus*	rose of Sharon sourwood *Hypericum* shrubby spp. Amur maple fruit peegee hydrangea*
Week 2 (8th - 14th)				
	pearly everlasting* *Ligularia* 'Desdemona' *Sedum rosea* Lobelia x speciosa		cup plant ironweed grape leaf anemone *Helianthus x multiflorus** butterfly bush*	scholar tree blue mist caryopteris
Week 3 (15th - 21st)				
Gentian septemfida plumbago	oriental lily, late varieties garlic chives		spearmint Helen's flower boneset*	Europ. mountain ash fruit Amer. cranberry viburn. fruit crabapple fruit
Week 4 (22nd - end)				
fall ladies tresses	perennial ageratum *Sedum* 'Vera Jameson' *Astilbe c. pumila*		turtlehead* tall goldenrods fountain grass *Physostegia virginiana** blue bush clematis	*Aralia spinosa*

12 8 Months of Color

SEPTEMBER

	PERENNIALS & BULBS		VINES, SHRUBS & TREES
Short	**Medium**	**Tall**	
Week 1 (1st - 7th)			
	Tricyrtis formosana showy stonecrop* gaura **Solidago spathulata**	Japanese anemone* *Aster* species* *Lespedeza thunbergii* *Eupatorium* species, late	silver fleece vine*
Week 2 (8th - 14th)			
		Aconitum napellus Japanese fleece flower **Helianthus divaricatus** *Miscanthus* 'Purpurescens'	Heptacodium micinoides
Week 3 (15th - 21st)			
October daphne	**Japanese wax bell** Weyrich mum Brazilian sage	ravenna grass **bluestem goldenrod** Indian switchgrass boltonia	fall clematis Virginia creeper leaf
Week 4 (22nd - end)			
		Miscanthus 'Zebrinus'	flowering dogwood leaf graystem dogwood leaf **honey locust leaf** staghorn sumac sugar maple leaf burning bush leaf Amur maple leaf

8 Months of Color

OCTOBER

PERENNIALS & BULBS			VINES, SHRUBS & TREES
Short	**Medium**	**Tall**	
Week 1 (1st - 7th)			
Colchicum species	hardy hybrid mum *Aster laterifolius* New England aster	Carmichael monkshood New York aster *Helianthus salicifolius*	red maple leaf tulip poplar leaf ash leaf serviceberry leaf aspen leaf sassafras doublefile viburnum leaf crabapple leaf hickory leaf hawthorn fruit & leaf
Week 2 (8th - 14th)			
	Tricyrtis hirta	*Miscanthus* species	larch leaf sweet gum leaf black gum leaf white oak leaf gingko leaf yellowwood leaf Boston ivy leaf bald cypress leaf
Week 3 & 4 (15th - end)			
Crocus kotschyanus	*Cimicifuga ramosa* Nippon mum		grape vine leaf summersweet clethra leaf witchhazel low-grow sumac leaf dwarf fothergilla leaf black locust leaf silver maple leaf linden leaf
Even Later (into November)			stewartia leaf American smokebush leaf arrowwood viburnum leaf poison ivy leaf Bumalda spirea leaf American witchhazel Norway maple leaf callery pear leaf paperbark maple

PLANT DESCRIPTIONS

Plant Names
On the Calendar and here in Plant Descriptions, you will find plants listed in alphabetical order by their half-month of peak bloom. You'll notice there are a mix of common and scientific plant names. Scientific names are uncomfortable for some gardeners, so common names are listed wherever possible. As an example, since the common name dwarf astilbe applies to both the early blooming Astilbe simplicifolia and the late A. chinensis pumila, it could cause confusion by appearing on two different calendars. In such cases I listed the plant by scientific name.

Cultural Information Notes
Within each plant description are keys to help you grow that plant successfully.

Light Requirements
    S   Sun. Minimum 6 hours direct sun per day.
    HS Half sun (also called half shade). 4 to 6 hours direct sun per day.
    Sh Shade. 2 to 4 hours direct sun per day.
    DS Dense shade. 0 to 2 hours direct sun per day.
    Where a range of light is indicated, such as "S to HS" the condition listed first is the better situation.

Soil Condition
    MWD Moist, well-drained soil. Soil that can hold moisture for several days but is never waterlogged.
    W   Wet soil preferred. Soil may sometimes be flooded during the growing season.

    "Tolerates" The species will grow in the stated situation but bloom, plant size, growth rate, stem strength, or overall health may be reduced.

Hardiness Zone
All of the plants on this calendar are hardy in USDA Zone 5 and of course they are also hardy in Zone 6. A few may not perform well in the warmest parts of Zone 7 and some are not reliably hardy in Zone 4. I don't specify the zone for each plant, however. That's because I understood when I first started to garden that these numbers are only approximations and my experience over the years has borne this out. Through ignorance or defiance of zone ratings, gardeners have and continue to disprove them. We order and successfully grow species we "shouldn't" and sometimes find that plants that "should" winter for us, don't.

Some authorities have taken these working revisions into account, while others ignore them. Thus, gardening publications disagree about many plants' cold hardiness. Some advise, "grow what you will and then tell the rest of us because this system is actually still new and developing." My own experience and input from gardeners in other zones confirm the practicality of this latter approach. For instance, while I was developing the material for this book, I saw plants rated not hardy in zone 4, appearing on peak bloom lists submitted by zone 4 correspondents. When I contacted those gardeners to question whether they might be growing such species with special winter protection, the answer was often a confused pause or a laugh, followed by, "No, I've grown it for years. You mean I'm not supposed to be able to?!"

So grow any of these plants you will. If in buying or ordering a plant you hear at your garden center, or by catalog zone rating, that it may need special protection, do that or not as you choose. The fun is in the growing, after all!

EARLY MARCH PEAK BLOOM

snow crocus (Crocus minimus) 3-4" tall flowers in mid-March, followed by grassy foliage; yellow, white, purple. S to HS. MWD soil.

snowdrops (Galanthus nivalis) white bells, 5-6" tall, April; dormant by summer. S to Sh. MWD soil.

spring witchhazel (Hamamelis vernalis and Hamamelis mollis hybrids such as 'Arnold's Promise,' 'Diana,' and 'Jelena') 10' tall, shrubby to 10' wide; branches covered with small, yellow to yellow-orange, fragrant flowers in February-March; good butter yellow or apricot fall color. HS to S, tolerates Sh. MWD soil.

winter aconite, aconite - (Eranthis hyemalis) yellow cupped flowers with delicate fringe-like leaves, mid-March, 4-6". S to Sh. MWD soil.

LATE MARCH PEAK BLOOM

contorted hazel, twisted filbert, Harry Lauder's walking stick (Corylus avellana 'Contorta') character shrub with twisted branches, gives it the look of a sculpture in winter; yellow catkin flowers hang from the branches in March-April; 8-10' tall and wide (easily kept smaller with annual removal of whole branches which can be used for decoration). S to HS. MWD soil.

cornelian cherry (Cornus mas) - multi-stemmed or low-branched tree, yellow flowers in March-April are like a toned-down, more dependably floriferous forsythia; June fruit eaten by birds, good fall color, 15-20' x 15-20'. S to HS. MWD soil.

Dutch crocus, crocus Dutch hybrids (Crocus chrysanthus) 6" tall flowers in late March, followed by grassy foliage; yellow, white, purple. S to HS. MWD soil.

Iris reticulata, mini iris, dwarf bulb iris (Iris reticulata) 4" tall flowers in March, blue, yellow, white or combinations of these colors; leaves grow after the flower is done blooming, look quite grassy and may be 15" tall (leaves go dormant and dis appear during the summer). S to HS. MWD soil.

Lenten rose (Helleborus x orientalis) showy mauve, white, or pink flowers in March like single peonies in clusters; false petals surrounding each flower last for well over a month, quite attractive; large deep green evergreen leaves; 12-18". HS. MWD soil.

silver maple, soft maple, white maple, river maple (Acer saccharinum) large, rounded tree, very fast growth rate often 18 - 24" per year, yellow fall color (leaves) 60-90' tall and 40-60' wide; clusters of yellow green flowers open in spring before leaves grow; these are not showy but important early food source for beneficial insects. S. MWD soil.

skunk cabbage, polecat weed (Symplocarpus foetidus) coarse 12-18" leaves in shady wet areas are the most notable feature; petal-less flower in March resembles a round mace inside a hood; flower known to melt its way through snow to bloom; crushed foliage and roots have skunky odor. HS to Sh. W soil.

squill (Scilla sibirica) blue starry flowers in late March - early April, grassy foliage dormant by midsummer, 6". S to Sh. MWD soil.

sugar maple, hard maple, rock maple (Acer sac charum) large, oval-spreading tree, medium growth rate, good red/yellow/orange color in fall (leaves) 75' tall and 50' wide; clusters of yellow green flowers open in spring before leaves grow; as with silver maple and many shade trees, this tree produces flowers that are not showy but important as food for beneficial insects. S to HS. MWD soil.

viola, pansy (Viola hybrids) 6" flowers, largest of the Violas, often with contrasting "faces". Flowers in all colors and combinations. Blooms in cool weather in spring and fall. Leaves may be evergreen. S to HS. MWD soil.

EARLY APRIL PEAK BLOOM

Adonis, pheasant's eye, Amur adonis (Adonis amurensis) 12-18" perennial with 2" golden flowers in April; attractive divided foliage. HS to Sh. MWD soil.

Draba (Draba Haynaldii) tiny alpine, 2" tall yellow flowers in April, tiny, narrow-grassy leaves in basal rosettes. S. MWD soil.

early daffodils (Narcissus hybrid such as February Gold) yellow and white trumpets, April to early May, 12". S to HS. MWD soil.

puschkinia (Puschkinia scillioides) charming spring bulb, 4-6" tall stalk with April flowers like hanging blue or white bells, each petal with a subtle contrasting stripe; dormant by summer. S to HS. MWD soil.

red maple, scarlet maple, soft maple, swamp maple (Acer rubrum) large, upright-spreading tree, medium- to fast growth rate, good red color in fall (leaves) and spring (clusters of April flowers not individually significant, give a red cast to whole tree); 50' tall and wide. S. MWD soil.

tarda tulip (Tulipa daysystemon) 4-5" tulips, bright yellow flowers, some with white outer petals, flowers open wide to flat in response to light and warmth, early blooming (April to early May) attractive seed pods. S to HS. MWD soil.

Tulipa turkestanica, multi-flowered tulip (Tulipa turkestanica) 12" flower stalks with dangling yellow and white flowers tinged with green; April. S to HS. MWD soil.

wild violet, horned violet (Viola cornuta) common lawn weed with many cultivated hybrids; 3-6" mound of heart shaped dark green leaves; violet flowers in April to May (hybrids may be white, red-violet or yellow); spreads rapidly by seed. S to Sh. MWD soil.

LATE APRIL PEAK BLOOM

Aubrieta deltoidea, false rock cress (Aubrieta deltoidea) blue green furry foliage forms an evergreen mat, violet, pink or white bloom in late April into May, 3". S to HS. MWD soil.

Dutch hyacinth, garden hyacinth, common hyacinth (Hyacinthus orientalis) very fragrant April flowers in 8" columnar cluster, varieties available in all colors. S to HS. MWD soil.

Dutchman's breeches (Dicentra cucullaria) 10" mound of ferny foliage, white flowers for a brief, beautiful period in April like white pantaloons hanging on a line; native North American woodland wildflower; distinguished from Dicentra canadensis - squirrel corn - by the yellowish tinge to flowers while squirrel corn has purplish tinge. Sh to HS. MWD soil.

dwarf Fothergilla (Fothergilla gardenii) - slender, crooked, often spreading branches, dense mound at maturity, slow grower, 2'-4' in height, similar or greater in spread; white, fragrant flowers April to early May appear before leaves. S to HS. MWD soil. Tolerates Sh and W.

forsythia, upright form (Forsythia x intermedia) - 8' round mound, yellow flowers in April; weeping forsythia (Forsythia suspensa) - sprawling, weeping 8' mound, yellow flowers in April. S to HS. MWD soil. Tolerates Sh.

Greigii tulips (Tulipa Greigii hybrids) 12-15" tulips, April bloom, leaves may be attractively mottled with maroon. Flowers range from yellow to orange to red and all shades between. S to HS. MWD soil.

hepatica, liverwort, sharp-leafed liverwort (Hepatica acutiloba) woodland wildflower native to North America, violet flowers may be blue or pink by site, 6", April; low evergreen leaves. HS to Sh. MWD soil.

Japanese andromeda (Pieris japonica or P. floribunda hybrid) broadleaf evergreen, new foliage dark red in spring after flowers fade; white flowers in late April like lily-of-the-valley; flowers buds showy all winter; 6' x 4', grows slowly. HS to S. MWD soil. Protect from wind and winter sun.

8 Months of Color   17

Kaufmaniana tulips (Tulipa Kaufmaniana hybrids) 12-15" tulips, many with water-lily shaped flowers; late April bloom. S to HS. MWD soil.

marsh marigold, cowslip, meadow-bright, kingcup, May-blob (Caltha palustris) large round leaves and bright yellow flowers in April-May; very decorative along pond edges and in the shallow water; goes dormant in summer. S to HS. W soil.

ornamental cherry, including **weeping cherry, weeping yoshino cherry** (Prunus species and hybrids). S to HS. MWD soil.
• P. sargenti - upright tree to 40', glossy red-brown bark, disease resistant; white April flowers
• P x yedoensis 'Yoshino Pink Form' - graceful weeping tree with pink flowers in late April to early May, glossy red-brown bark in winter also attractive;15-20' x 15-20' at maturity, may be kept smaller with annual pruning (variety called 'Snow Fountain' has white flowers)

pasque flower, windflower (Anemone pulsatilla, syn. Pulsatilla vulgaris) purple, burgundy or white flowers in April persist long into May, delicate fluff seed pods in June, ferny mound of foliage throughout summer; 8". S. MWD soil.

primula, primrose (Primula x polyantha) clusters of flowers on 6" stems above puckered, evergreen leaves in a basal rosette; flowers in every color and bi-colors; blooms in cool weather of spring and fall, primary bloom period April and early May. S to HS. MWD soil. Tolerates Sh.

Pulmonaria saccharata, Bethlehem sage, lungwort, boys and girls, hundreds and thousands (Pulmonaria saccharata) Large leaves with silvery gray spots, rosy buds that open into violet blue flowers in May; 12". HS to Sh. MWD soil. Tolerates dry soil.

spring beauty (Claytonia virginica) tiny plant carpets shady areas in April with pink flowers, goes dormant by June. Sh to HS. MWD soil.

star magnolia (Magnolia stellata) low branched, shrub-like tree, white-pink flowers open wide and starry, come in April before the large leathery leaves, attractive grey bark; 10-15' x 10-15'. S to HS. MWD soil. Tolerates shade.

EARLY MAY PEAK BLOOM

ajuga (Ajuga repens varieties) evergreen ground-hugger, 6" blue spike flowers in May, colorful leaves on many varieties. HS. MWD soil. Tolerates S and Sh.

Anemone blanda, wood anemone, Grecian windflower (Anemone blanda) mounded plant with white, pink or blue flowers in April-May; 3-6". HS to S or Sh, best in HS. MWD soil.

Anemone sylvestris, European woods anemone (Anemone sylvestris) white open-faced flowers 18", spreads by runner. HS to S. MWD soil.

apricot (Prunus armeniaca) 20' spreading tree, white flowers in May, edible fruit, yellow fall color sometimes good. S to HS. MWD soil.

bergenia (Bergenia cordifolia) 8" large evergreen leaf like a single thick cabbage leaf, dark glossy green during growing season, maroon in winter; rose flowers on 15" stalk in May. HS to Sh or S. MWD soil. Tolerates dry soil.

bleeding heart (Dicentra spectabilis) mound of divided foliage, romantic heart-shaped flowers on arching branches May-June, goes dormant late summer; 2-3'. HS. MWD soil.

Brunnera macrophylla, bigleaf forget-me-not (Brunnera macrophylla) large puckered foliage with light blue flowers May into June; 15". HS. MWD soil.

callery pear, flowering pear (Pyrus calleryana) white flowers in April or early May, good fall color, fast growth. S to HS. MWD soil.

celandine poppy (Stylophorum diphyllum) grey-green leaf, yellow flowers in May, 20" (Very similar to Chelidonium majus. Chelidonium is supposedly more weedy, taller -at 4' - and leaves on Chelidonium are deeply pinnatifid rather than Stylophorum's pinnately lobed leaf. Stylophorum has a bristly seed capsule while Chelidonium has a cylindrical seed capsule.) HS to Sh. MWD soil.

clove currant (Ribes odoratum) native North American shrub with fragrant yellow flowers shortly after forsythia - early May; 6-8' tall and round. S to HS. MWD soil. Tolerates Sh.

creeping phlox (Phlox subulata) evergreen mat of foliage, carpet of white, lavender or pink flowers in May; 3". S. MWD soil. Tolerates HS

cushion spurge (Euphorbia polychroma) mounded yellow-green foliage all summer, bright yellow flowers in May, good fall color, distinctive mounded shape; 2'. S. MWD soil.

daffodil (Narcissus species or hybrid such as variety King Alfred or Dutch Master) yellow, white or bicolor trumpet-shaped flowers in May; range of heights from 4 - 24". S to HS. MWD soil.

epimedium spp., bishop's hat (Epimedium species) semi-evergreen groundcover, heart shaped leaves on wiry 6" stems, white, red or yellow flowers in May. HS to Sh. MWD soil.

foamflower (Tiarella cordifolia) grey-green foliage like small furry maple leaves, white starry spikes of flowers in late April or early May, nearly evergreen; 8". HS to Sh. MWD soil. Clump-forming foamflower (Tiarella cordifolia 'Wherryi') leaf, flower and height as in species; leafier leaf clusters; clump-forming, does not spread by runners like the species.

fringed bleeding heart (Dicentra eximia) ferny blue-green foliage, dangling heart-shaped flowers in abundance in May and June, sporadically throughout summer; 18". HS. MWD soil.

grape hyacinth (Muscari armeniacum) blue violet flowers like inverted clusters of grapes in early May, foliage goes dormant in July, reappears in fall, 6" stalks. S to HS. MWD soil.

koreanspice viburnum (Viburnum carlesii)rounded, dense shrub, 4-5' x 4-8', white flowers late April to early May, outstanding fragrance. S to HS. MWD soil. Tolerates Sh.

large-flowered comfrey (Symphytum grandiflorum) dense colonizer, yellow white flowers 12" tall in May, large leaves attractive all summer. S to HS. MWD soil. Tolerates dry soil.

large-flowered trillium, trillium (Trillium grandiflorum) classic wildflower, 3-petal showy white flowers in May; 12-15". HS to Sh or S. MWD soil.

leopardsbane (Doronicum caucasicum) daisy-like yellow flower in May-June; nice mounded foliage; 12". HS. MWD soil.

merry bells (Uvularia grandiflora) curiously drooping yellow-green bells on 12" plant, May; N. American native. HS to Sh. MWD soil.

mid-season tulip (Tulipa hybrids) May flowers, all colors and combinations, 18-24". S. MWD soil.

Money plant, honesty (Lunaria annua) biennial, white or purple flowers in May-June, papery white half-dollar seed pods in fall, self sows, 3-4'.

myrtle euphorbia (Euphorbia myrsinites) prostrate, blue-green, heavily textured plant, semi-evergreen; flowers yellow-green in May; grown primarily for foliage and texture effect. S to HS. MWD soil. Tolerates Sh and dry soil.

myrtle, periwinkle (Vinca minor) evergreen vining groundcover, violet, white and red flowers in May. S to Sh. MWD soil.

8 Months of Color

perennial alyssum (Aurinia saxatilis) evergreen gray-green foliage in a 12" mat; branches sprawl along ground to 3' length; 18" flower stalks bear fragrant yellow, gold or apricot flowers in May. S. MWD soil. Tolerates dry soil.

perennial candytuft, candytuft (Iberis sempervirens) a mound of bright white flowers in May, dense evergreen, 10". S to HS. MWD soil.

PJM rhododendron, early rhododendron (Rhododendron hybrids) broadleaf evergreen, smaller leaf than many later rhodos, pink-purple flowers in May, size varies with site and pruning. HS to S. MWD soil. Protect from wind and winter sun.

quince S to HS. MWD soil. tolerates Sh and dry soil.
  • dwarf quince (Chaenomeles japonica) - densely branched mound, salmon or rose flowers in May; 3' x 4'
  • flowering quince (Chaenomeles speciosa) dense branched thorny shrub, rose, salmon, or white flowers in May, 6' x 6'.

redbud (Cercis canadensis) - pink or white flowers in late April-early May, interesting dark bark shows orange undertones in furrows with age; 20' x 25'. HS to S. MWD soil. Tolerates Sh.

rock cress (Arabis caucasica, Arabis blepharophylla other Arabis species) evergreen gray-ish foliage in a low mat, flowers white on 6-12" stalks in May. S to HS. MWD soil.

saucer magnolia (Magnolia x soulangiana) low branched small tree, decked with white, pink or purple flowers in April or early May before the leaves emerge (flower color varies with cultivar); attractive grey bark; up to 25' tall and wide, depending on variety. S to HS. MWD soil. Tolerates Sh.

serviceberry, shad, shadblow, juneberry (Amelanchier canadensis) - smooth grey bark, white fragrant late April-early May flowers, reddish fruit in June for birds, apricot fall color; 15-25' spreading tree. HS to S. MWD soil. Tolerates Sh and W soil.
  • running serviceberry (Amelanchier stolonifera) shrub, bark, flower, fruit and fall color like the tree; forms dense clumps 5-8' tall. HS to S. MWD soil. Tolerates Sh and W soil.

summer snowflake (Leucojum Gravetye) bulb plant, 18-24" tall, white bell-like flower in May. S to Sh. MWD soil.

sweet woodruff (Galium odoratum) spring green whorled foliage attractive all summer, scented like new-mown hay, starry white flowers in May; 8". HS to S or Sh. MWD soil.

toothwort, pepperroot (Dentaria diphylla) white-pink flowers in loose cluster at top of 10" stalk, foliage divided; North American native of moist woods, dormant by mid summer. HS to Sh. MWD soil. Tolerates W soil.

trout lily, dogtooth violet (Erythronium canadensis) 6-9" flower stalk with down-turned yellow flower like a tiny turk's cap lily; speckled leaves; woodland wildflower blooms in early May. Sh to HS. MWD soil.

woodland phlox (Phlox stolonifera) semi-evergreen creeping plant, oval dark green leaves cover the ground 4-6" deep, light blue flowers held in clusters several inches above the leaves in May. HS to Sh. MWD soil. Tolerates S.

LATE MAY PEAK BLOOM
alpine aster (Aster alpinus) blue or pink daisy-like flowers on 12" stems over a mat of dark green foliage. S to HS, MWD soil

alpine currant (Ribes alpinum) 3 - 6' in height and usually as wide; densely twiggy rounded shrub; greenish yellow flowers not very showy; yellow fall color. S to HS. MWD soil.

American cranberry viburnum, American cranberrybush (Viburnum trilobum) 8-10' rounded shrub, white flowers in May, red berries persist through winter, good fall color. S to HS. MWD soil. Tolerates Sh and wet soil.

Amur honeysuckle, Tatarian honeysuckle (Lonicera tatarica) shrub honeysuckle that was long a mainstay of backyard hedges and fence rows; fragrant pink to white-pink flowers in May-June on ascending, arching stems, sometimes outstanding; 8-12' tall and wide. S to HS. MWD soil. Tolerates Sh.

bridal wreath spirea (Spiraea prunifolia) old fashioned upright spirea blooms earliest of its genus, button-like double white flowers smother the stems in May; fall color is often good orange-bronze; 6-9' tall, somewhat narrower than tall but suckers to form thick colonies. S to HS. MWD soil.

Burkwood viburnum (Viburnum x Burkwoodii) evergreen or semi-evergreen shrub, 6' x 6', white hemispherical flower clusters touched with pink in May; very fragrant. HS to S. MWD soil. Tolerates Sh.

Calycanthus floridus, sweetshrub, Carolina allspice, pineapple shrub, strawberry shrub (Calycanthus floridus) suckering shrub, to 10' tall, dark red to red-brown flowers in May; all parts of the plant fragrant with scent like strawberry. S to HS. MWD soil.

Camassia cusickii, camas, Indian quamash (Camassia cusickii) bulb plant, 18" spears of starry blue or white flowers in May; wide-grassy foliage dormant by mid summer; North American native, of moist meadows. S to HS. W to MWD soil.

Canada anemone (Anemone canadensis) Bright white poppy like flowers May-June, leaves like a crow's foot, colonizes; 1'-2'. HS to Sh. MWD soil.

Carolina silverbell, silverbell (Halesia carolina) small round tree, 30' tall, white bell flowers hang in clusters in May. HS. MWD soil.

catmint (Nepeta Mussinii) fragrant grey mounded foliage, lavender-blue or white flowers May-June and sporadically through summer; 12"-18". S to HS. MWD soil. Tolerates dry soil.

columbine (Aquilegia many species and hybrids) rounded blue green leaves on wiry stems, cupped flowers in many colors with backward flaring spurs, June; height varies by species, from 1'-3'. HS to S. MWD soil. Tolerates Sh.

common lilac, lilac (Syringa vulgaris hybrids) - 10' or taller shrub, fragrant violet, white or pink flowers in May-June. S to HS. MWD soil.

crabapple (Malus hybrids and varieties) vast assortment of sizes from 6' to 30', some weeping; white, pink or mauve flowers in May; foliage on some has maroon cast; red or yellow fruit, on many is highly ornamental; some varieties hold fruit well into winter; fall color occasionally good yellow. S to HS. MWD soil.

creeping soapwort, soapwort (Saponaria ocymoides) evergreen mat-former, 6", May-June pink flowers. S. MWD soil.

culinary sage (Salvia officinalis, including varieties with variegated or other-colored leaves) semi-evergreen, 18" tall, violet flowers in spikes, May-June. S. MWD soil.

dame's rocket, sweet rocket (Hesperis matronalis) 3' erect plant, violet or white clustered flowers in May-June. Biennial to weakly perennial. S to Sh. MWD soil.

Dianthus species. S to HS. MWD soil.
  • Maiden Pinks (Dianthus deltoides and hybrids) mat forming rich green foliage, deep rose colored flowers May-June 6" stalks

Dutchman's pipe vine (Aristolochia durior) fast growing vine with huge round leaves, old fashioned screen for a front porch; yellow-green flowers have shape and size of tobacco pipe, May bloom, spreads to 30'. S to HS. MWD soil. tolerates Sh.

dwarf bearded iris (Iris germanica, dwarf hybrids) sword shape foliage, showy lowers of many colors in May; 6-12". S to HS. MWD soil.

8 Months of Color

Euphorbia griffithii, fireglow euphorbia (Euphorbia griffithii 'Fireglow') ferny leaves, pink-tinged green, 2-3' stems with yellow green flowers framed by red-orange bracts, May-June. S to HS. MWD soil.

European cranberry viburnum (Viburnum opulus) 10-12' fast growing shrub, white lacecap flowers in May quite showy, red fruit ripens in early fall, very attractive. S to HS. MWD soil.

Exbury azalea, deciduous azalea (Rhododendron hybrids, those of the 'Northern Lights' series esp. good for zone 5, such as 'Rosy Lights,' 'White Lights,' 'Yellow,' etc.) 4-5 narrow, vase-shaped shrub, huge fragrant, white, pink, orange or yellow flowers for Mother's Day each May, coarse foliage a nice contrast to finer textures in summer; dependable performer. HS to S. MWD soil.

flowering dogwood (Cornus florida) - white or pink flowers in May, graceful horizontal branching habit, good maroon fall color; 20' x 20'. HS to S. MWD soil. Tolerates Sh.

gas plant (Dictamnus purpureus) rose or white starry flowers in spikes, late May or early June, sturdy columnar plant, deep green foliage, attractive seed pods in July-August, 3'. S to HS. MWD soil.

geum (Geum coccinea, many varieties available such as 'Mrs. Bradshaw') orange flowers on 6" stems, May-June. S to HS. MWD soil.

heucherella (x Heucherella tiarelloides) neat 6" mound of evergreen foliage; 15-18" wiry, leafless stems hold tiny pink bells in May-June. HS to S; tolerates Sh. MWD soil.

horsechestnut (Aesculus hippocastanum) large tree, 50' or more, coarse foliage, large white flowers in conical clusters in late May. S to HS. MWD soil.

late tulip (Tulipa varieties, late season bloom such as Parrot and lily-flowered types) array of colors, flowers in late May on stems 18-36". S. MWD soil.

lily of the valley (Convallaria majalis) fragrant white bells on a wiry stalk in May; 6-8" leaves are a summer groundcover. HS to Sh. MWD soil. Tolerates Sh and dry soil.

mountain bluet (Centaurea montana) deep blue flower on 12-24" stem in May-June; mound of lance shaped leaves is ragged after bloom, if cut back hard blooms again in August. S to HS. MWD soil.

mouse-ear forget-me-not, forget-me-not (Myosotis biennis) sky blue flowers in May - June; biennial: allow seedlings to sprout; 6". S to Sh. MWD soil.

nannyberry viburnum, sheepberry (Viburnum lentago) large shrub or small tree, 15-20'; creamy white flowers in flat-topped clusters, May; blue-black berries in July-August can be attractive as they ripen, when green, pink and blue-black berries are all together. S to HS. MWD soil.

oxeye daisy, field daisy (Leucanthemum superbum, syn. Chrysanthemum leucanthemum) 18-24" white daisies in late May, sometimes repeat mid-summer. S to HS. MWD soil.

perennial geranium - many species come into bloom together: (HS to S. MWD soil. Tolerates Sh.)
- pink perennial geranium (Geranium endressi 'Claridge Druce') light flowers May-June, a mounded plant with fragrant leaves; 15-18"
- double geranium (Geranium himalayense 'Plenum') Double purple-blue flowers May-June above a mound of large leaves.
- bigroot perennial geranium (Geranium macrorrhizum) pink flowers May-June, a few blooms here and there throughout summer, foliage has a nice coppery fall color and is fragrant; 12"
- wild perennial geranium (Geranium maculatum) pink flowers May-June, peaks bloom earlier than most cultivated species, naturalizes rapidly, foliage has a nice coppery fall color; 12"
- dark-eyed perennial geranium (Geranium psilostemon) magenta flowers with dark veins, May-June, 18", may bloom again in August

- blood-red geranium (Geranium sanguineum) red-violet flowers May-June, foliage has a nice coppery fall color; 15"
- geranium Ballerina (Geranium cinereum 'Ballerina') lilac-pink flowers with dark center and purple veining, long blooming May-July, 4-6"
- geranium Johnson's Blue (Geranium x 'Johnson's Blue') purple-blue flowers May-June above a mound of large leaves.

potentilla, herbaceous species, dwarf potentilla. S to HS. MWD soil.
- Potentilla verna nana compacta syn. Potentilla tabernaemontani compacta - mounded 3-4" perennial, yellow flowers in May-June
- Potentilla nepalensis (var. 'Miss Willmott' well known) - loose cluster of strawberry-like foliage 6-10", flowers salmon to rose-pink on 10-12" stalks in May-June
- Potentilla alba - foliage like strawberry, flowers white in May, 6-10"

red field poppy (Papaver atlanticum) red or red-orange flowers on 2' stems in May, grey-green hairy foliage dormant by July; spreads aggressively. S to HS. MWD soil.

red horsechestnut (Aesculus x carnea) rose-pink flowers in May-June, very large leaves make tree quite coarse in texture, a round tree to about 20', usually less. S to HS. MWD soil.

redtwig dogwood (Cornus alba sibirica) best known for red twigs in winter, 8' x 12'; flowers white on old stems, blue berries in midsummer favored by birds - but flower and fruit usually not present because shrub is normally pruned hard to encourage new red stems
- Cornus alba sibirica 'Elegantissima' - white edged leaves. S to HS. MWD to W soil.

sargent crabapple (Malus x sargentii) - 6' tall, 10' wide tree, white flowers in late May follow pink buds, red fruit persists through winter. S to HS. MWD soil.

sea pinks (Armeria maritima) dense rounded evergreen mat 3-4" tall pink blooms in May June. S. MWD soil.

Siberian pea shrub/tree, weeping pea (Caragana arborescens and C. a. 'Pendula') erect, narrow shrub, taller than broad with hanging clusters of yellow flowers in May, 15 to 20' tall x 12 to 18'. S to HS. MWD soil. Very adaptable. Seed pods make a popping sound as the pods open in July/August. C. a. 'Pendula is a narrow weeping tree, with other characteristics same as for the species.

slender deutzia (Deutzia gracilis) white flowers pack the branches in May, shrub is otherwise unremarkable; 2-6' tall, 3-4' wide. S to HS. MWD soil. Tolerates Sh and dry soil.

snowball viburnum (Viburnum opulus 'Sterilis') 10-12' fast growing shrub, white pom-pom flowers in May quite showy, no fruit (sterile flowers only). S to HS. MWD soil.

star of Bethlehem (Ornithogalum nutans) 18-24" bulb plant, white flowers in loose hemispherical clusters in May-June; dormant by mid summer; spreads readily. S to Sh. MWD soil.

swamp buttercup (Ranunculus acris) 2' plant with yellow buttercups in May and June; inner surface of petals highly reflective, gleaming; foliage can be kept neat and plant continuing to bloom into July and even August by continuous deadheading. S to HS. MWD to W soil.

Trollius, globeflower
(Trollius europaeus) turban-type bright yellow or yellow-orange flowers in May-June, sporadically throughout summer; 15". S to HS. MWD soil.

Vanhoutte spirea, snowmound spirea
(Spiraea vanhouttei) - white flowers in dense clusters along arching stems in May - June, fall color can be good, 8' tall x 8' wide. S to HS. MWD soil.

8 Months of Color

verbascum, purple mullein (Verbascum phoeniceum) large pebbled leaves lie flat, flower stalk is 2-5' tall with pink, purple or white flowers in May-June; many hybrids exist, some hybrids bloom for extended periods. S to HS. MWD soil.

vernal sweet pea (Lathyrus vernus) 1' neatly erect plant, pink flowers in May. HS to Sh. MWD soil.

Veronica prostrata, creeping veronica (Veronica prostrata) ground-hugging mat of semi-evergreen foliage, 2" blue spikes May-June. S to HS. MWD soil.

Virginia bluebells (Mertensia virginica) 18" stems tipped with pink buds opening into blue dangling floral bells in May; dormant by July. HS. MWD soil.

white baneberry, doll's eyes (Actaea pachypoda) 18-24" bushy plant with large leaves, white flowers at the tips of branches in May; white fruit with dark spot at base in July resembles a doll's eye (do not eat - toxic). HS to Sh. MWD soil.

willow amsonia, amsonia (Amsonia tabernaemontana) 3' upright plant, dense lacy leaves, sky-blue flowers in large clusters top the plant in May; frequently the fall color is a warm gold. HS to S. MWD soil. Tolerates Sh and dry soil.

EARLY JUNE PEAK BLOOM

allium species, Height and color varies by species and variety. Additional species and many hybrids exist. S to HS. MWD soil.

medium varieties, 1 to 3' -
- A. caeruleum (blue)
- A. aflatunense (violet)
- A. Christophii (violet)
- A. globosum (pink)
- A. pulchellum (yellow/green to rose)

short varieties. -
- sunny twinkles (Allium moly) yellow flowers on 6" stalks in June, dormant later in summer
- rose allium (Allium ostrowskianum) rose colored flowers in June, dormant later in summer; 6"
- white flowering onion (Allium neopolitanum) white flowers in June, summer dormancy; 6"

alternate leaf dogwood, Pagoda dogwood (Cornus alternifolia) horizontally spreading tree 25' tall by 25' wide or wider; yellow-white flowers in fuzzy clusters in early June, very fragrant; berries ripen from green to red to blue-black in July, eaten by birds. HS to S. MWD soil. Tolerates Sh.

American elderberry (Sambucus canadensis) coarse, rather gangly shrub native to moist meadows and wetlands of North America; white flat-topped cluster flowers in June; blue black berries in August are edible (wine, pies) and attractive to birds; 10-12' tall and wide. S to Sh. MWD to W soil.

amur maple (Acer ginnala) - multi-stemmed or low-branched tree, good rusty fall color, 25' x 20'; June flowers are insignificant but necessary to seed pod color of pink in July-August; take care not to spray insecticides while it's in bloom or pollinators will be killed. S to HS. MWD soil.

angelica (Angelica archangelica) biennial, huge bright green leaves are attractive, 5 stalks with dill-green flowers in globes steal the show in its second year, self-sows. S to HS. MWD soil.

arrowwood viburnum (Viburnum dentatum) - upright spreading shrub, white lace-cap flowers in May, blue berries in June eaten by birds, plum or russet fall color; 10-12' x 6'. S to HS. MWD soil. Tolerates Sh.

autumn olive (Elaeagnus umbellata) spreading silver-green shrub, 12' x 12' or larger, greenish-yellow fragrant flowers in late May or early June, edible berries prize by small mammals and birds. S to HS. MWD soil, tolerates dry soil.

beauty bush (Kolkwitzia amabilis) 8-10' arching shrub, fragrant pink flowers in June. S to HS, tolerates Sh. MWD soil

black locust, common locust, yellow locust, white locust (Robinia pseudoacacia) rough barked large tree usually very high branched with upper branches sinuous in outline; June flowers in pendant white clusters very fragrant; no significant fall color. S to HS. MWD soil

blue fescue, sheep's fescue (Festuca ovina glauca) 8" evergreen grass, silvery-blue, wheat-like tops to 18" in June. S to HS. MWD soil

blue oat grass (Helictotrichon sempervirens) nearly evergreen blue-green clump grass, interesting wheaty seed heads in June; 2'. S to HS. MWD soil

blue-eyed grass (Sisyrinchium angustifolium) grassy iris relative native to moist sunny areas of east North America; tiny blue-violet iris-like flowers in May-June; 8-18". S to HS. MWD to wet soil

Bowles golden grass (Carex stricta 'Bowles Golden') a sedge, dense tuft; fine leaf blades are glowing yellow-green, 12"; greenish flower not significant, in June. HS to Sh, MWD soil.

Centaurea dealbata, Persian cornflower (Centaurea dealbata) mound of divided, lance-shaped leaves; pink-purple flowers 18" tall in June. S to HS. MWD soil, tolerates dry soil.

cheddar pinks (Dianthus gratianopolitanus) 2" mat of evergreen blue green foliage, brilliant pink or red-violet flowers on 6-8" stalks in June. S to HS. MWD soil

climbing hydrangea (Hydrangea anomala petiolaris) glossy round leaves, large white lace-cap flowers in late May or early June; can grow on walls and tree trunks without support, up to 40'; honey-colored exfoliating bark attractive in winter. S to HS, tolerates Sh. MWD soil

clustered bellflower (Campanula glomerata) cluster of basal foliage produces 1-3' stems with smaller leaves and densely clustered blue or white flowers in June; C. glomerata acaulis has flowers on very short stalks, barely rising above foliage. S to HS. MWD soil

common privet - hedge shrub often overlooked and flowers not seen if kept severely trimmed; golden vicary privet more often recognized (Ligustrum x Golden Vicary) dense, upright, multi-stemmed shrub with yellow-green foliage, new foliage bright yellow; creamy white flowers in May-June, black fruit in September-October. 10-12' high and wide. S to HS. MWD soil, tolerates dry soil.

common thyme, mother of thyme, English thyme (Thymus serpyllum) fragrant grey mat-forming plant, pink flowers in June, 2-3". S. MWD soil

coral bells (Heuchera sanguinea) neat foliage in a 6" mound, sprays of red, pink or white flowers in June to 18"; nearly evergreen. S to HS, tolerates shade. MWD soil

Cotoneaster species. S to HS. MWD soil

- creeping cotoneaster (Cotoneaster adpressus) 12-18" horizontally branching shrub, pink or white flowers in June, red berries persist into winter; good groundcover: roots and spreads where branches make good contact with soil
- cranberry cotoneaster (Cotoneaster apiculatus) 3' spreading shrub 3-6' wide, whitish-pink flowers in June, berries eaten by birds or may be present in fall for a time; round in outline
- spreading cotoneaster (Cotoneaster divaricatus) hedge type shrub, 6-8' tall and wide, round in outline; pink flowers in June; fruit in fall can be attractive but often hidden by foliage and then gone to birds and small mammals by leaf-fall

Crambe cordifolia, crambe (Crambe cordifolia) impressive 6' flower stalks in July are leafless; white flowers in masses are sweet scented; huge, rough-surfaced basal foliage. S. MWD soil

Crambe maritima, sea crambe (Crambe maritima) large, wide-ruffle blue-green foliage to 12", honey-fragrant white flowers in masses on leafless 18" stalks in June. S. MWD soil

creeping baby's breath (Gypsophila repens) white flowers In June; 6". S. Soil must be very well drained.

creeping forget-me-not (Myosotis scorpioides) mat of foliage with light blue flowers May-September; 2-3"; native to moist, shaded stream-sides, eastern North America. HS, to Sh or S. MWD to wet soil.

cut-leaf stephanandra (Stephanandra incisa) groundcover shrub 4-7' tall, with graceful arching branches and lacy foliage; white flowers in June; variety 'Crispa' most frequently used, grows only 18-30" tall. HS to S or Sh. MWD soil

Dianthus species. S to HS. MWD soil.
- pinks (Dianthus alpinus) 2" mat of evergreen foliage, brilliant white, pink or crimson flowers on 4" stalks in June
- cottage pinks (Dianthus plumarius) blue-green evergreen grassy 12" foliage, white, pink or red fragrant flowers in June on 18" stalks
- Allwood hybrid pinks (Dianthus x alwoodii) grassy blue-green foliage 6-8", flowers in many colors on 12" stems beginning in June, continuing sporadically through summer

doublefile viburnum (Viburnum plicatum tomentosum) - spreading shrub with sculptural horizontal habit, white lace-cap flowers in late May or early June in double file along every branch, red berries in July eaten by birds, plum or russet fall color; 10' x 10'. S to HS. MWD soil

dropwort, meadowsweet (Filipendula vulgaris, syn. Filipendula hexapetala) Boston-fern foliage and Queen Anne's lace white flower in June; 18" mound of foliage, 3' flower stalk. S to HS, tolerates Sh. MWD soil.

dwarf lilac (Syringa patula 'Miss Kim') 4-6' tall and wide, fragrant violet flowers in late May or early June; leaves smaller than and flowers in smaller clusters than common lilac. S to HS. MWD soil.

early ladies tresses, common ladies' tresses, nodding ladies tresses (Spiranthes cernuum) orchid native to moist sunny places in North America; endangered in much of its range, including Michigan; translucent 12-20" stems bear ghostly white down-turned flowers in June-July; foliage is basal. S to HS. MWD to wet soil.

European mountain ash (Sorbus aucuparia) small tree, 25-35'; rounded in outline; June white flowers in flat, dense clusters are showy, as are the clusters of orange to orange-red fruit in August that stay into fall until the birds eat them all; divided leaves give feathery appearance. S to HS. MWD soil.

false indigo (Baptisia australis) large columnar plant, often mistaken for shrub, blue flowers along stem ends in late May-June; interesting black, persistent seed pod in fall; 4', slow to grow. S to HS, tolerates Sh. MWD soil.

firethorn, pyracantha (Pyracantha coccinea) - thorny evergreen, white flowers in late May or early June, orange fruit in fall, upright habit, can be espaliered for narrow vertical feature; 6-18'. S, tolerates HS and Sh. MWD soil, tolerates dry soil.

foxglove (Digitalis purpureus) biennial, spire-like plant 3-5' tall, purple, white, yellow or pink flowers shaped like glove tips hang down one side of tall flowering stalk June-August; first year (non-blooming year) leaves are low and large like a hosta; must be allowed to set seed and seedlings must be allowed to sprout to perpetuate itself. HS to S or Sh. MWD soil.

foxtail lily (Eremurus himalaicus) basal foliage like yucca but not stiff; naked flower stalk to 4'; has white, yellow or pink flowers in June in dense spear-head cluster up to 2' long; dormant by midsummer. S to HS. MWD soil.

giant allium, giant flowering onion (Allium giganteum) a large sphere of purple flowers in June on a straight 3' stalk. S to HS. MWD soil.

8 Months of Color

golden chain tree (Laburnum x watererii) small tree to 20', round in outline; pendulous clusters of yellow flowers in June; seeds toxic. S to HS. MWD soil

hawthorn species. S. MWD soil, tolerates dry soil:
- cockspur hawthorn (Crataegus crusgalli) 20', low branched shrubby tree often used as a hedge; extreme thorniness makes an impenetrable barrier; May white flowers; fruit in summer eaten by wildlife
- English hawthorn (Crataegus laevigata) round or columnar small tree, 20' tall; white malodorous flowers in May (pink in some varieties such as 'Paul's Scarlet' and 'Crimson Cloud'); red fruit ripens in early fall, eaten by birds
- Lavalle hawthorn (Crataegus x Lavallei) 15-25' round tree, with thorns, white flowers in late May or early June; good coppery red fall color; brick red fruit may persist into winter

honey locust (Gleditsia triacanthos) flat-topped spreading tree 40-60', fast growing; fragrant white flowers in pendant clusters in June; seed pods -telltale flat pods of the pea family - may persist into winter and maybe messy. Popular thornless, golden-foliage type is flowerless and seedless often confused with black locust. S to HS. MWD soil.

Iceland poppy (Papaver nudicaule) small, fuzzy foliage clustered at base of plant; delicate leafless stems rise to 18"; large, pastel colored flowers with petals like crepe paper; short lived perennial, often treated as a biennial; self sows readily in a favorable site S to HS. MWD soil.

iris, bearded types (Iris germanica hybrids) sword shape foliage, showy flowers of many colors in May or early June; 2-3'. S to HS. MWD soil.

Irish moss (Arenaria verna caespitosa) moss-like 2-3" tall carpet plant, tiny white flowers in June, refreshing spring-green foliage is evergreen, nice for between stones HS. MWD soil.

Jacob's Ladder (Polemonium caeruleum) columnar to vase shaped, blue or white flowers in late May or early June, 18-24". HS to S. MWD soil.

Japanese kerria (Kerria japonica) - round shrub, dense branched, green twigs in winter, yellow flowers like single or double roses in May, again in August if cut after June bloom; 6'. S to HS, tolerates Sh. MWD soil.

Korean lilac, palibin lilac, dwarf lilac (Syringa meyeri) 4-6' tall and wide, violet flowers in May, fragrant. S to HS. MWD soil.

kousa dogwood (Cornus kousa) - starry white or pink flowers in June, ruddy pink fruit in July, good coppery fall color, bark becomes three-color as it ages; 20' x 20'. HS to S. MWD soil.

lady's mantle (Alchemilla mollis, A. vulgaris and related dwarf species A. alpina) mounded grey-green foliage with yellow-green foamy flowers in May-June; foliage 12", flower stems 18"; round leaves of full-sized species catch and hold moisture prettily in individual glistening drops; A. alpina foliage lobed, edged with silver hairs that lend a variegated look. HS to Sh or S. MWD soil.

large-flowered clematis, clematis, Virgin's bower (Clematis hybrid) Showy star shaped white, purpleor red flowers, 8' vine needs support; June -July bloom. S to HS. MWD soil.

lemon lily (Hemerocallis Lilioasphodelus) 3' fragrant yellow daylily; trumpet flowers bloom in June ahead of most cultivated varieties. S to HS. MWD soil.

lupine (Lupinus hybrids) violet, pink, white or yellow flowers in spike arrangement; 3'; June; blue-green leaves are round but divided like umbrella spokes, quite attractive. S to HS. MWD soil.

meadow rue, thalictrum HS to S or Sh. MWD soil.
- columbine meadow rue (Thalictrum aquilegifolium) tiny yellow green flowers in sprays in June; colonizes in open woods area; in formal garden needs to be staked in May; 4'.
- lavender mist meadow rue (Thalictrum rochebrunianum) columbine like foliage; delicate sprays of lavender flowers in June-July; 3'

8 Months of Color

Milfoil yarrow, thousand-leaf yarrow (Achillea millefolium) 18-24" tight flat cluster of white, pink or red-tone flowers in June, ferny foliage low to the ground. S. MWD soil, tolerates dry soil.

mock orange (Philadelphus x virginicus) - white fragrant flowers like single roses ranged along the stems in June, narrow upright shrub to 15' tall; double-flowered and dwarf forms exist. S to HS, tolerates Sh. MWD soil.

mouse-ear coreopsis (Coreopsis auriculata) tight mound of foliage 12-15", yellow daisy-like flowers in June 18-24"; dwarf form 'Nana' is 12" including flower. S to HS. MWD soil.

Nectaroscordum siculum - bulb, narrow grassy leaves at the base, naked flower stalk lifts flowers to 4'; flowers are greenish-purple in June, resemble a large globe allium except flower stalks are pendulous - the whole cluster of flowers appear to droop from the tip of the flower stalk; seed capsules very interesting and upright in contrast to "drooping" flowers. S to HS. MWD soil.

ninebark (Physocarpus opulifolius) rounded shrub much like the better known snowmound spirea in shape, texture and size; white flower fading to pink in May and June, reddish fruit in September, 5' or more. S to HS. MWD soil.

oriental poppy (Papaver orientale) large frilly flowers in red tones, pink and white, June, ferny foliage goes dormant in July; 3'. S to HS. MWD soil.

ornamental rhubarb (Rheum palmatum varieties) enormous basal leaves emerge maroon, mature to green with maroon underside; red seed pods on 6' stems in June. S to HS. MWD soil.

painted daisy (Chrysanthemum coccineum) 2' tall daisy flowers in June may be white, red, pink, yellow; foliage fern like; rather a sloppy plant but well loved for cut flowers. S to HS. MWD soil.

pea vetch, American vetch, purple vetch (Vicia americana) native wildflower of moist meadows; purple-pink pea-like flowers in June and sporadically through summer; stems may be 3' long but rarely so tall, as prefers to scramble along the ground or twine and lean on other plants. S to HS. MWD to wet soil.

peony (Paeonia lactiflora) large white, red or pink flowers in late May-June, rarely yellow flowers; 3'-4' dark green leafy plant. S to HS. MWD soil.

perennial gladiola (Gladiolus byzantinus) 18" spike with sword-like leaves, in June trumpet-like flowers along one side of the stem are rose, white, or bi-color; dormant by August. S to HS. MWD soil.

Phlox ovata, mountain phlox (Phlox ovata) large-leaf groundcover phlox, oval leaves to 6"; pink or purple flowers on 20" stems, sometimes white flowered forms appear; June bloom. S to HS. MWD soil.

Polygonum Bistorta, bistort, snakeweed (Polygonum Bistorta) large basal leaves like spinach or dock, nearly-naked flower stems 18-24" tall with white flowers clustered at the tip to give the appearance of a wand; flowers age to pink; invasive in its preferred moist habitat; variety 'Superbum' is taller, with denser flower clusters. S to HS, tolerates Sh. MWD to wet soil.

potentilla, shrubby species (Potentilla fruticosa variety) - 2-4' twiggy shrub, yellow, white, orange-yellow or pink-salmon flowers all summer. S to HS. MWD soil, tolerates dry soil.

prairie smoke, old man's whiskers, Johnny smoke (Geum triflorum) native wildflower of Midwest and Canadian prairies, muted flesh tone or orange-purple flower in June; plume like wisps on July seed pods; 12"; long, divided, basal leaves are attractive through summer. S to HS. MWD soil.

pussy's toes, ladies' tobacco, everlasting (Antennaria dioica) creeping grey-leaf wildflower native to sunny, well-drained areas in North America; "furry" white or pink flowers in clusters on naked 6" stems in June resemble a cat's paw with claws retracted; pink form A. dioica rosea. S. MWD to dry soil.

red baneberry (Actaea rubra) white bottlebrush flowers at the tips of branches in late May or early June; bushy plant 18"; fruit is brilliant red in July (and toxic). HS to Sh. MWD soil.

Robinia x ambigua, ornamental locust, lilac locust, violet pea tree (Robinia x ambigua) small tree to 15 or 20'; pink or rose-violet flowers coat the stems in June, obviously pea family flowers. S to HS. MWD soil.

rodgersia (Rodgersia species) dramatic large leaves, white flowers in June, 18". HS to Sh, tolerates S if soil constantly wet during growing season. MWD soil.

salvia species. S to HS. MWD soil.
- Salvia grandiflora - pin-purple, lilac, sometimes white flowers on 40" stems in June-July
- blue sage (Salvia azurea) stems hold spike clusters of deep blue flowers above large, somewhat furry leaves in June; 18" and taller

salvia superba, perennial salvia (Salvia x superba) 15-24" spikes of purple in June, again in July if cut after first bloom; pebbly surface grey-green foliage. S to HS. MWD soil.

sedum, short early species such as below. S to HS. MWD soil.
- sedum 'Gold Carpet' (Sedum acre 'Gold Carpet') yellow June flower, lime green mossy foliage, 4"
- orange stonecrop (Sedum kamschaticum) succulent-leaf groundcover, attractive coppery color in fall, orange bloom in June, 6"

self-heal (Prunella vulgaris, P. v. laciniata) field weed of Europe naturalized in U.S. and cultivated in its large-flowered and cut-leaf forms; basal foliage in mound to 6", thimble-shaped flower clusters in June and sporadically through summer; pink-purple petals on stems 8-12" tall; invasive by seed. S to HS, tolerates Sh. MWD to wet soil.

Siberian iris (Iris sibirica) grassy 3' foliage, May or early June flowers in violets, white, yellows. S to HS, tolerates Sh. MWD to wet soil.

snow in summer (Cerastium tomentosum) bright white flowers in June on mounds of 6" ever-grey foliage. S to HS, tolerates Sh. MWD soil, tolerates dry soil.

Solomon's seal. HS to Sh. MWD soil.
- Solomon's seal (Polygonatum biflorum) strongly arching stems mature at 3-4' tall, creamy white flowers dangle in pairs from bottom of arch in May-June, followed by paired berries
- variegated Solomon's seal (Polygonatum odoratum variegatum) strongly arching stems mature at 2' tall, striking white edged leaves; creamy white flowers dangle from bottom of arch in May-June, followed by white berries

spiderwort (Tradescantia virginiana) 20-30" grassy-leaf plant with violet-purple, blue-violet or white flowers late spring to mid summer. S to HS, tolerates Sh. MWD soil.

strawberry (Fragaria virginiana hybrid) 6" groundcover with white (pink on some varieties) flowers in May, edible red fruit in June. S to HS. MWD soil.

sweet bay magnolia (Magnolia virginiana) large leaf and repeat bloom make this magnolia especially nice; large, scented white flowers open May - August; 10-20' wide and tall. S to HS. MWD soil.

sweet William (Dianthus barbatus) red, pink, white or bi-colored flowers in May continuing into July if kept deadheaded; 18-24"; biennial, so allow some seed to set and seedlings to grow. S to HS. MWD soil.

tree lilac, Japanese tree lilac (Syringa reticulata) oval-round small tree 20-30' tall and somewhat narrower; fragrant white flowers in June later than common lilac; glossy cherry-like bark. S to HS. MWD soil.

8 Months of Color

tulip poplar, tulip tree (Liriodendron tulipifera) very large tree with curious flat-tipped leaves; green "tulips" marked with salmon and cream open in June; best viewed from upper floors of a home or looking down on a tree growing on lower ground, since flowers are often missed when the tree is viewed from its base. S to HS. MWD soil.

Valeriana officinalis, valerian, garden heliotrope (Valeriana officinalis) white fragrant flowers on 2-3' stems in June. S to HS. MWD soil.

weigela (Weigela florida) - arching branches in a 6'-9' mound, red, white or pink flowers in June repeat sporadically through summer; dwarf and variegated forms smaller than species. S to HS, tolerates Sh. MWD soil.

wisteria (Wisteria chinensis hybrids) large vine which can climb a support or be trained to a tree form, has dangling purple, rose or white clusters like grapes in June; to 75'. S to HS. MWD soil.

yellow flag iris, yellow sweet flag (Iris pseudacorus, I. p. variegata) striking 4-5' sword-like foliage, cream-striped in the variegated form; butter yellow flower in May; naturalized in U.S. wetlands but native to Europe and North Africa. S to HS, tolerates Sh. Wet to MWD soil.

yellow hawkweed, hawkweed (Hieracium species) native North American wildflowers with hairy basal leaves; flowers on leafless or nearly leafless stems, tufted orange (H. aurantiacum - July, 12-15") or yellow (H. umbellatum - June, 20"). S to HS. MWD soil.

LATE JUNE PEAK BLOOM

Achillea taygetea , silvery-leaf yarrow- dissected silver-green foliage, flat-topped light yellow flowers in June; 18"; one of the parents of the popular variety 'Moonshine' and lends its early-blooming characteristic to that variety. S to HS. MWD soil.

Anacyclus (Anacyclus depressus) short lived perennial or biennial with ferny, ground hugging leaves and white daisy flowers in June-July. S to HS. MWD soil.

Astrantia species. HS to S, tolerates Sh. MWD soil.
- masterwort (Astrantia major, white or Astrantia carniolica, rose) pretty foliage and white cutting and drying flowers in June; 2'
- rose masterwort (Astrantia major rubra or Astrantia carniolica) pretty foliage and good rose pink cutting and drying flowers in June; 2'

biennial blackeye Susan (Rudbeckia fulgida) yellow daisy-shape flowers with dark centers in June-August; native North American biennial or short-lived perennial; hairy leaves distinguish it from its most famous offspring, 'Goldsturm'; 3'. S to HS. MWD soil.

birdsfoot trefoil (Lotus corniculatus) golden yellow flowers from late June through summer on ferny mounded 12-18" plant; often seen along roadsides - naturalized in the U.S. from Europe. S. MWD soil, tolerates dry soil.

blue flax, flax (Linum perenne) light blue or white flowers May-July like a cloud; 24". S to HS. MWD soil.

blue fringed bleeding heart (Corydalis flexuosa) ferny blue-green foliage, light blue flowers abundant in June, 15". HS to Sh. MWD soil.

bottlebrush buckeye (Aesculus parviflora) horse chestnut like leaf, white candle like flowers in July-August; 8-10' and sometimes taller. HS to S or Sh. MWD soil.

bull thistle (Cirsium vulgare) 4-5' biennial, native to sunny fields; flowers in very large purple tufts late June - early August; seeds loved by birds. S to HS. MWD soil.

Carolina lupine (Thermopsis caroliniana) 4-5' leafy, upright perennial with yellow pea-family flowers at the tips of the branches in June. S to HS. MWD soil.

Carpathian harebell, blue clips/white clips bellfower (Campanula carpatica; varieties 'Blue Clips' 'White Clips' very common) 6" mounds of bright green foliage with sprays of 10" flower stalks; blue-violet or white bells on wiry stems in June-July, will repeat bloom if kept deadheaded. S to HS. MWD soil.

Clematis recta - 5-6' perennial, shrub like with support, but sprawling on its own; small leaves smoky or purplish in some varieties; small white flowers in profusion in June-July. HS to S. MWD soil.

Clematis viticella, late clematis - small-flowered (2-3"), late blooming 8-9' vine; flowers white, blue-violet or lilac; may be cut to the ground annually without disturbing bloom. HS to S. MWD soil.

common harebell, bluebells of Scotland, varied-leaf harebell (Campanula rotundifolia) small, dark green round leaves mound up in spring to 6", disappear by summer leaving only the wiry flower stalks with narrow lance leaves and blue or white bell shaped flowers; 6-18" native around the globe in north 40's latitude. S to HS. MWD soil.

Corydalis lutea, golden bleeding heart, yellow fumitory (Corydalis lutea) ferny blue green foliage in delicate mound 12" tall, golden flowers in June, naturalizes where conditions are favorable and in naturalized state young plants which flower a bit later - July - are always in abundance to extend the blooming season. HS to Sh. MWD soil.

crown vetch (Coronilla varia) straggle-branched pea family plant frequently (mistakenly) used as an erosion control groundcover; pink flowers in June; tiny leaves on 18" tall mat. S to HS. MWD soil.

delphinium (Delphinium elatum) tall wands of blue, white or violet-tone flowers in June-July above a mound of maple-like foliage; 4-5'. S to HS. MWD soil.

Digitalis species. HS to Sh or S. MWD soil.:
• perennial foxglove (Digitalis mertonensis) 3' perennial, spike of raspberry-colored flowers in June-July
• yellow foxglove (Digitalis ambigua) 3' perennial, spike of yellow flowers in June-July; flowers smaller but more numerous than standard foxglove
• perennial yellow foxglove (Digitalis lutea) pale yellow, small flowers dangle on 3-4' spike in June-July

dwarf spirea (Spiraea x bumalda 'Gold Flame,' 'Anthony Waterer' and S. japonica varieties such as 'Princess') - 2-3' round shrub, dense twiggy, pink, white or red flowers in June-July will repeat in August if shrub is sheared immediately after first flowers begin to fade; can be cut down to stubs every year, will grow back to full size and flower that same year; varieties 'Gold Flame,' 'Gold Mound', and 'Lime Mound' have orange foliage in spring and fall, yellow-green foliage in summer. S to HS. MWD soil.

early astilbe hybrids (Astilbe x arendsii) ferny foliage 1'-3' high, blooms white, red, pink or mauve upright plumes or arching sprays in June-July. There are early (late June), mid (early July) and late (mid-late July) blooming varieties.

early and repeat-blooming daylily varieties (most famous - Hemerocallis Stella D'oro) 2 or 3 periods of bloom, June - fall; trumpet like flowers in many colors; 12-48". S to HS. MWD soil.

early Lilium, hybrid lily, oriental lily (Lilium hybrids) trumpet flowers in late June or July (varies by variety), whorled foliage on tall stems; 2-4'. S to HS. MWD soil.

feverfew (Chrysanthemum parthenium) white button flowers in June-July; fragrant foliage; 15-18". S to HS. MWD soil.

fireweed, great willow-herb, wickup (Epilobium angustifolium) 4-5" column topped with distinctly pointed spikes of purple flowers in July, species is fast spreading; white form slower; native to disturbed areas in eastern North America. S. MWD soil.

8 Months of Color

Gaillardia species, blanket flower (esp. Gaillardia x grandiflora) - 2' mounded plant; daisy-shaped flowers with showy, concentric bands of yellow, orange and red; blooms late June or July to August; repeats bloom into fall if kept deadheaded; dwarf and single-color varieties exist. S. MWD soil, tolerates dry soil.

Geranium dalmaticum, Dalmation geranium - rose-pink flowers in June; mounded 12" plant of round leaves rather smaller than other perennial geraniums; foliage has good coppery-red fall color. HS to S. MWD soil.

goatsbeard, child of two worlds (Aruncus dioicus) ferny leaf, white-green flower plume in June; 4'. HS to S or Sh. MWD soil.

golden Marguerite (Anthemis tinctoria) yellow daisy flowers 3-4' tall from June to end of July, longer if kept deadheaded; short-lived perennial requires annual division. S. MWD soil.

graystem dogwood (Cornus racemosa) native suckering shrub, 10-15' tall; forms large colonies in fields and woods edge; white lacy clusters bloom in June; white berries in August eaten by birds; good purple fall color. HS to Sh or S. MWD soil.

Heckrott honeysuckle, vine honeysuckle (Lonicera x Heckrottii) pink and yellow trumpet flowers late June to frost, blue green leaves, vine can twine on supports to 15' or more. HS to S, tolerates Sh. MWD soil.

hosta, early blooming species: Hosta undulata varieties such as 'Albo-marginata'; and some hybrids of H. sieboldiana such as 'Elegans' and 'Great Expectations'. Beautiful vari-colored foliage is the attraction. The white or pale lilac flowers are beautiful to some, attractive to hummingbirds, but clipped off as a distraction to foliage by some gardeners. Sh to HS. MWD soil.

hosta, mid-season blooming species (and representative varieties): Hosta decorata; H. hypoleuca; H. nakaiana (such as 'Candy Heart', 'Blue Boy', 'Blue Cadet', 'Golden Tiara'); H. sieboldiana (some varieties); H. tardiana group (such as 'Krossa Regal'); H. venusta. Beautiful vari-colored foliage is the attraction. The purple/violet or pale lilac flowers are beautiful to some, attractive to hummingbirds, but clipped off as a distraction to foliage by some gardeners. Sh to HS. MWD soil.

Iris pallida - 18-24" iris with pale blue-violet flowers in June; variegated form I. pallida 'Aureo variegata' has yellow stripe up each leaf; zebra iris I. pallida variegata has white-striped foliage. S to HS. MWD soil.

Japanese iris (Iris Kaempferi) 3' grassy, erect plant, late June flowers in wide range of colors open flatter than Siberian or blue flag iris. S to HS. MWD soil.

Jasione perennis, sheep's bit - mat of small light green leaves, 12" sky blue flowers in profusion in June. S to HS. MWD soil.

knautia macedonica tuft of foliage 6-10"; red-purple flowers on 12-15" stems in June, sporadically through summer; short-lived perennial. S to HS. MWD soil.

lamb's ears (Stachys lanata) woolly grey foliage, 18-24" tall mauve flowers on grey furry stalks in June-July need to be removed after flowering is done to maintain groundcover effect. S to HS. MWD soil, tolerates dry soil.

lanceleaf coreopsis (Coreopsis lanceolata) in June and July 10-48" flower stalks hold bright yellow daisy-like flowers above bright green foliage only 1/3 the height. S to HS. MWD soil.

lemon thyme (Thymus x citriodorus) evergreen, tiny leaf perennial with the scent of lemon; pinkish flowers in June; 6-12"; varieties Silver Queen and Aureus white variegated and golden thymes, respectively. S, tolerates HS. MWD soil, tolerates dry soil.

linden. S to HS. MWD soil.
- **littleleaf linden** (Tilia cordata) pyramidal shape and densely branched; bark is gray brown ridged; 60 to 70' in height and 1/2 to 1/3 that in spread; yellow fall color

8 Months of Color

- basswood (Tilia americana) forest tree sometimes planted as shade tree, 50', oval in outline; masses of fragrant white flowers in June; golden in fall

Lysimachia punctata, spotted loosestrife, yellow loosestrife - 3-4' leafy, perennial with sizable yellow-green flower at the base of each leaf in June-July; aggressive colonizer. HS to S, tolerates Sh. MWD soil.

Missouri primrose (Oenethera missouriensis) sprawling 8-12" plant with big yellow flowers that unfurl like full skirts from red-speckled long-pointed buds; June, sporadically through summer. S, tolerates HS. MWD soil.

northern catalpa, hardy catalpa (Catalpa speciosa) 50' irregularly oval tree with large leaves and unmistakable "cigar" seed pods that hang after leaves fall; fragrant white flowers in conical upright clusters in June. S to HS. MWD soil.

Oenethera caespitosa, evening-flowered primrose - 6" mound with large rose flowers in June; flowers are fragrant, open at night, close by morning (other Oenethera share the common name evening-flowered primrose). S, tolerates HS. MWD soil.

Oenethera speciosa, pink primrose (Oenethera speciosa/rosea) pink flowers June-July, 18-24", fast spreading. S to HS. MWD soil.

Penstemon species, beardtongue S, tolerates HS. MWD soil.
- many Penstemon species and varieties bear white, pink and red flowers in early summer; flowers arrayed on stalks like a snapdragon's; from 12-36"; attractive to hummingbirds: P. hirsutus, P. digitalis, P. nitidus, P. pinifolius often seen but dozens of species have been taken into cultivation, hybridized extensively in Europe, and re-introduced to the U.S.; most native to North America
- husker red penstemon (Penstemon x digitalis 'Husker Red') maroon leaves spring and fall, 3' stalks of white flowers June-July followed by maroon seedheads

perennial sweet pea (Lathyrus latifolius) 8" groundcover or 8' vining plant, rose pink or white flowers in June-July, often carry on into August. S to HS. MWD soil.

pincushion flower (Scabiosa caucasica) airy plant; white, pink or blue frilled daisy flowers on 30" stems June - August. S to HS. MWD soil.

Polygonum affine, border jewel, Himalayan fleeceflower - mat forming ground cover, white flowers on 9" spikes become bright rose seed pods, bloom begins in June continues all summer; semievergreen. S to HS, tolerates Sh. MWD to wet soil.

Potentilla atrosanguinea, scarlet cinquefoil - 8-12" plant with grey leaf; scarlet red flowers in June. S, tolerates HS. MWD soil, tolerates dry soil.

Rosa multiflora, pasture rose, multiflora rose (Rosa multiflora) clusters of small, single, white flowers in June on a suckering, invasive shrub naturalized throughout the U.S.; tiny dark red rose hips in fall are attractive, persist into winter. S to HS. MWD soil, tolerates dry soil.

Salvia verticillata, lilac sage, purple meadow sage (Salvia verticillata) lilac blue flowers whorled around a 3' spike in June. S to HS. MWD soil.

Scabiosa 'Butterfly Blue' a dwarf pincushion flower (Scabiosa columbaria) blue frilled daisy flowers on 15" stems June-August. S to HS. MWD soil.

scarlet campion (Lychnis coronaria) semi-ever-grey plant, 6-8" of mounded leaves, 15-18" of erect flower stalks, brilliant red-violet flowers June-July. S, tolerates HS. MWD to dry soil.

swordleaf inula (Inula ensifolia) yellow daisy-like flowers in late June-July, neat, mounded 18-24" plant. S to HS. MWD soil.

8 Months of Color

threadleaf coreopsis (Coreopsis verticillata) tiny leaves give an airy appearance, small daisy-like yellow flowers across the top of a 24" plant June-July; 'Moonbeam' is pastel yellow, 18", later to bloom and long-blooming; 'Zagreb' is shorter at 15", with more gold colored flowers; Golden Showers is gold, with a shorter blooming season. S to HS. MWD soil.

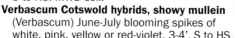

Verbascum Cotswold hybrids, showy mullein (Verbascum) June-July blooming spikes of white, pink, yellow or red-violet, 3-4'. S to HS. MWD soil.

veronica species. S to HS. MWD soil.:
- grey veronica (Veronica incana) spikes of blue flowers in June-July above a grey carpet of foliage, semi-evergreen; 12"
- spike speedwell, veronica (Veronica spicata) spikes of white, pink or blue flowers in June-July; 18"
- Veronica subsessilis - spikes of blue flowers in June-July, 18-24"; attractive deep green, glossy foliage

vine euonymus (Euonymus fortunei radicans) shrubby upright broadleaf evergreen, can be trained to vine up to 15'; insignificant greenish-white flowers in June followed in some varieties by yellow orange fruits for fall decoration. HS to Sh or S. MWD soil.

Virginia sweetspire (Itea virginica) native suckering shrub with fragrant white bottlebrush flowers in June; excellent glowing red fall color. HS to S, tolerates Sh. MWD soil.

Washington hawthorn (Crataegus phaenopyrum) round, densely branched tree, thorny, good purple color to new foliage in spring, orange to red in fall, white flowers in June; red berry-size fruit hangs on over winter, eaten by birds in spring; 20-25'. S. MWD to dry soil.

winterberry, Michigan holly (Ilex verticillata -one male such as 'Apollo' needed in the area to pollinate fruit-bearing females; 'Sparkleberry' a good full-size female form) dark green foliage, insignificant white flowers along the stems in June; bright red fruit ripening in late August, persisting into January. HS to Sh or S. MWD to wet soil.

wood lily (Lilium philadelphicum) 2-3' up-facing red-orange flowers speckled maroon in June; native in much of the upper Midwest and East of North America. HS to Sh. MWD soil.

yellow yarrow, fernleaf yarrow (Achillea filipendulina and hybrids) leaves like Boston fern are fragrant, grey-green; flat tight clusters of yellow flowers in June-July; variety 'Moonshine' earliest to bloom; height variable up to 4'. S, tolerates HS. MWD soil.

EARLY JULY PEAK BLOOM

Astilbe simplicifolia (Astilbe simplicifolia) 10-12" high, neat shiny toothed foliage and arching sprays of pale pink to pure white flowers in July. HS to Sh and S if very moist. MWD soil.

baby's breath (Gypsophila paniculata) white or pink flowering airy plant; 3' round in July bloom. S. Soil must be very well drained.

bear's breeches, spiny bear's breeches (Acanthus spinosissimus) impressive large thistle-like foliage, but shiny; 3' flower spike has elegant white and purple-tinged flowers. HS to S or Sh. MWD soil.

bee balm (Monarda didyma) - 3' erect plant, leaves and flowers fragrant, pink, red white or violet flowers in July. HS, tolerates S or Sh. MWD soil.

blue linaria, blue toadflax, blue wild snapdragon (Linaria purpurea) grey-green tiny leaves on upright 18-24" plant; blue-violet flowers in spikes, July. S to HS. MWD soil.

Bupthalmum salicifolium, oxeye - large, rough foliage 18-24", large ragged-petal yellow daisy flowers in July rise to 36". S. MWD soil, tolerates dry soil.

butterfly weed (Asclepias tuberosa) orange or red flowers in y shaped clusters in July, vase shaped, attracts butterflies 18-24". S. MWD soil, tolerates dry soil.

buttonbush (Cephalanthus occidentalis) rangy, native North American wetlands shrub; 10-15'; July flowers are white globes like fuzzy golf balls; very fragrant. S to HS. Wet to MWD soil.

calamint (Calamintha Nepeta) fast spreading, pink-blooming herb; 2'; July bloom, repeats sporadically through summer. S to HS. MWD soil.

California hyacinth (Tritelia laxa, syn. Brodiaea laxa) unusual bulb plant, tall stems with funnel-shaped blue-violet flowers in June or early July, grassy foliage goes dormant in late summer; 18". S to HS. MWD soil.

chestnut, Chinese chestnut (Castanea mollissima) rounded 50' tree with sharply-toothed leaves; sprays of small white flowers in July. S to HS. MWD soil.

Chinese lantern, strawberry tomato, winter cherry (Physalis Alkekengi) 2' aggressively spreading plant; July flowers are small, green-white, not the feature for which the plant is grown; large bright orange seed pods in fall. S to HS. MWD soil.

Coreopsis rosea, pink threadleaf coreopsis - tiny leaves give an airy appearance, small pink daisy-like flowers across the top of the plant July-August; 15". S to HS. MWD soil.

Cupid's dart (Catananche caerulea) 24" short-lived perennial with sky blue papery-tuft flowers July-August; foliage mostly basal. S to HS. MWD soil.

dwarf goatsbeard (Aruncus aethusifolius) lacy leaf, white-green flower plume in late June-July; 12". HS to S or Sh. MWD soil.

early astilbe hybrids (Astilbe x arendsii) ferny foliage 1'-3' high, blooms white, red, pink or mauve upright plumes or arching sprays in June-July. There are early (late June), mid (early July) and late (mid-late July) blooming varieties.

Heliopsis scabra, false sunflower - yellow daisy shaped flowers on erect 3-4' plant, blooms June-August. S. MWD soil.

Heuchera x brizoides, coral bell varieties such as 'Palace Purple' - maroon to bronze maple-like foliage in a 12" mound; sprays of creamy white or tiny greenish flowers in July to 18"; nearly evergreen. HS to S, tolerates Sh. MWD soil.

hollyhock mallow (Malva Alcea) 2-3' narrow upright perennial with pink, rose or white flowers in July; spreads rapidly by seed. S to HS. MWD soil.

Hypericum calycinum, creeping St. Johnswort - semievergreen groundcover, olive-green foliage in 12" mounds, bright yellow flowers in July. S to HS. MWD to dry soil.

Hypericum, shrubby species. S to HS. MWD soil.
• shrubby St. Johnswort (Hypericum prolificum) 2-4' x 4' shrub, 1" gold flowers with furry centers in July
• kalm St. Johnswort (Hypericum kalmianum) 2-3' round shrub with narrow blue-green leaves, 2" yellow flowers with furry centers in July
• St. Johnswort (Hypericum densiflorum) 4 x 4 shrub with oval leaves, yellow flowers in July.
• creeping St. Johnswort (Hypericum calycinum) a 12-15" groundcover, semi-evergreen with large yellow flowers in late July and early August.

Jupiter's beard (Centranthus ruber) fragrant pink flowers (red and white varieties available) in dense conical clusters on 18-36" stems that prefer leaning or draping to standing upright. Great cascading over a wall. Self sows. S to HS, MWD soil.

lady bells (Adenophora liliifolia) 18" plant with hanging, pale violet bell flowers in July; aggressive spreader. S to HS. MWD soil.

lavender (Lavandula angustifolia) ever-grey subshrub, fragrant foliage and flowers, violet or white wands in June-July, 15-24". S. MWD to dry soil.

Lilium spp., mid-season Lilium, hybrid lily, oriental lily (Lilium hybrids) trumpet flowers in a wide range of colors and combinations, mainly white, pink, orange, yellow and red in July , whorled foliage on stems from 2-4'. S to HS, tolerates Sh. MWD soil.

Lysimachia ciliata loosestrife- 3-4' leafy perennial, fast to spread by underground runners; yellow flowers at base of upper leaves; July; in variety 'Purpurea' foliage is maroon in spring, less so in summer. HS to S, tolerates Sh. MWD soil.

Lysimachia ephemerum - silver loosestrife a medium textured, gray-green to blue-green foliageon a sturdy columnarplant 2-3' tall. White flowers on spikes peak in late July. S to HS, MWD soil.

Madonna lily (Lilium candidum) fragrant white lilies on very dark green to maroon stems. S to HS, MWD soil.

Maltese cross (Lychnis chalcedonica) very bright red-orange flowers in June - early July on columnar 3' plant; variety Vesuvius smaller, with maroon foliage. S to HS. MWD soil.

mid-season daylily varieties (Hemerocallis varieties) trumpet like flowers in July in many colors; 12-48" stems, wide-grassy leaves. S to HS. MWD soil.

oakleaf hydrangea (Hydrangea quercifolia) - white pointed clusters of flowers in July age to tan, persist through winter, large leaves cinnamon or maroon in fall; peeling bark; 3-5' x 4-5'. HS to S or Sh. MWD soil.

pale purple coneflower (Echinacea pallida) 4-5' pink-purple flowers have drooping long petals - badminton birdies; native to Great Plains of North America; butterflies attracted to the nectar, birds to the seeds. S to HS. MWD soil.

Phlomis russeliana (Phlomis russeliana) upright stems and broad gray-green leaves give this 3-4' plant great presence but yellow flowers tiered in dense whorls are even more eye catching. Sun, well drained soil.

queen of the meadow (Filipendula ulmaria) attractive sharp-edged leaves, clusters of tiny white flowers in June-July; 3'; variegated form exists. HS to S, tolerates Sh. MWD soil.

red hot poker, torch plant, poker plant (Kniphofia uvaria) sloppy, wide-grassy leaves sprout 3' naked stems that opens a poker of red-orange flower buds that open to yellow, giving the effect of a glowing torch. S to HS. MWD soil.

ribbon grass, gardener's garters (Phalaris arundinacea 'Picta') white-striped foliage, fast spreading grass, 24" leaves with sparse seed heads to 3' in early July. S to HS. MWD soil.

rocket ligularia (Ligularia stenocephala 'The Rocket') spires of sulphur-yellow flowers in July, large attractive leaves, 3-4'. HS to Sh. MWD soil.

Sanguisorba obtusa, burnet - ferny 18" mound of foliage; 24-30" stems bear white bottlebrush flowers that fade to pink in July; more attractive, less weedy than related white-flowering burnets S. canadensis and S. officinalis. S to HS. MWD soil.

sea holly (Eryngium planum and several similar species) blue-grey basal foliage, 3-4' near-leafless stems hold prickly-thimbles of steely blue or white flowers in July, each thimble with a ruff of sharp blue-grey bracts. S to HS. MWD soil, tolerates dry soil.

Serbian bellflower (Campanula poscharskyana) July-blooming, rambling purple bellflower up to 18" tall where it has a wall or taller plant to lean on; nearly evergreen. HS to Sh, tolerates S. MWD soil.

Shasta daisy (Leucanthemum superbum, syn. Chrysanthemum x superbum) classic white flowers in July; 3'; dwarf and double flowered varieties exist. S to HS. MWD soil.

Sidalcea spp., mini hollyhock (Sidalcea malviflora) spires of pink or rose flowers like tiny hollyhocks July-August, repeats bloom if kept cut back; 30". S to HS. MWD soil.

smoke tree. S to HS, tolerates Sh. MWD soil, tolerates dry soil.
  • smoke tree, smoke bush, Venetian sumac (Cotinus coggygria) shrub to small tree, 15'; large oval leaves with flattened tip; cream or pink flowers in plumes, July; fluffy seed pods ornamental into August; varieties with maroon foliage or weeping branches exist
  • American smoke tree, chittamwood (Cotinus obovata) small tree, 25-30'; large oval leaves with flattened tip; July flowers are insignificant; glowing orange fall color is a major asset

snowball hydrangea (Hydrangea arborescens) round clusters of white flowers in July-August; 3' mounded shrub. HS to S, tolerates Sh. MWD soil.

Stewartia pseudocamellia, Japanese stewartia - beautiful mottled bark, fragrant white flowers like old fashioned roses in July, good fall color from yellow to purple; 30' x 30'. S to HS. MWD soil.

sundrops primrose, day primrose (Oenethera tetragona) bright yellow flowers June-July from red buds, basal leaves evergreen (maroon in winter); 18". S to HS, tolerates Sh. MWD soil.

Ural false spirea (Sorbaria sorbifolia) ferny-leafed shrub, white plume flowers in July attractive to butterflies, good orange fall color; 4-8' x 4-5', suckers and spreads wider over time. S to HS, tolerates Sh. MWD soil.

yucca, Adam's needle (Yucca filamentosa) a coarse 2-3' mound of evergreen sword-shaped leaves, white flowers on impressive 4-8' stalk in June/early July. S to HS. MWD to dry soil.

LATE JULY PEAK BLOOM

Achillea The Pearl (Achillea ptarmica 'The Pearl') very aggressive; 18"; white-button flowers in July-August. S, tolerates HS. MWD soil.

Allium senescens, curly allium - lilac-pink globe flowers in July; 15". S to HS. MWD soil.

Anemone x robustissima summer windflower - handsome mounded foliage all summer, tall stems of white or pink poppy-like flowers late July to early August; 3-4'. S to HS, tolerates Sh. MWD soil.

Astilbe taquetii (Astilbe chinensis var. taquetti 'Purperkerze') spikes of purple-red flowers in late July and August, bronze-green foliage, 3'. HS to Sh, S if very moist. MWD soil.

balloon flower (Platycodon grandiflorus) starry blue-violet, white or pink flowers in July and August, deep green foliage; 36"; dwarf varieties exist. S to HS, tolerates Sh. MWD soil.

blackberry lily (Belamcanda chinensis) sword-haped foliage, 3' stalks of orange 1" trumpet like flowers in July-August, followed by pods that split to display shining black seeds in August-September. S to HS. MWD soil.

blue globe thistle (Echinops exaltatus) steely-green globes open into blue flowers in July-early August, grey-green foliage, 4'; seeds are a favorite food of goldfinches & chickadees. S to HS. MWD soil.

blue hydrangea, pink hydrangea, mophead and lacecap hydrangeas, bigleaf hydrangea (Hydrangea macrophylla hybrids and varieties) round clusters (mophead) or lacy flat clusters (lacecap) of pink, blue or red flowers in July-August, large dark green leaf; shrubs 3-5' tall and round. HS to S, tolerates Sh. MWD soil.

bouncing Bet (Saponaria officinalis) phlox-like flowers on 3' tall stems in July-August; pink or white. S to HS. MWD soil.

Cimicifuga racemosa, fairy candle (Cimicifuga racemosa) 3-6' wands of malodorous white flowers in July, ferny foliage. HS to Sh or S. MWD soil.

8 Months of Color

crocosmia (Crocosmia hybrid 'Lucifer') sword like foliage to 2', naked flower stalks 3-5' with arcs of bright red-orange flowers at the tips in July-early August; at the edge of its hardiness in USDA zone 5. S to HS. MWD soil.

culver's root (Veronicastrum virginicum) 3-4' erect plant with whorled foliage, white or pink pike flowers in July; native to moist meadows in eastern U.S. S to HS. MWD soil.

edelweiss (Leontopodium alpinum, syn. Gnaphalium leontopodium) grey-furry alpine, a rosette topped with downy white flowers in July to 6". S. MWD soil.

German statice (Goniolimon tataricum, syn. Limonium tataricum) basal foliage, naked flower stems to 18" with pink-white cloud of tiny, long-lasting flowers in July. S. MWD soil.

golden rain tree (Koelreuteria paniculata) 30-40'; yellow flower in July; papery cream-color seed pod that follows often mistaken for flower; leaves are purplish red when unfolding, bright green at maturity, sometimes yellow in fall. S to HS. MWD soil.

Goldsturm rudbeckia, perennial blackeye Susan (Rudbeckia fulgida 'Goldsturm') yellow daisy-shape flowers with dark centers in July-August, very dependable and vigorous; 2-3'. S to HS. MWD soil.

gooseneck loosestrife (Lysimachia clethroides) 3' columnar plant tipped with clusters of white flowers in July, flower cluster resembles a goose's head and beak. S to HS, tolerates Sh. MWD soil.

hoary vervain (Verbena hastata) 4', purple candelabra spikes in July. S to HS. MWD to wet soil.

hollyhock (Alcea rosea) spires of pink, red, yellpw, purple or white flowers July to September, large rounded leaves; 4'; biennial or weakly perennial; self-sows readily. S to HS. MWD soil.

hosta, mid-season blooming species (and representative varieties): Hosta decorata; H. hypoleuca; H. nakaiana (such as 'Candy Heart', 'Blue Boy', 'Blue Cadet', 'Golden Tiara'); H. sieboldiana (some varieties); H. tardiana group (such as 'Krossa Regal'); H. venusta. Beautiful foliage is the attraction. The white to shades of purple flowers are beautiful to some, attractive to hummingbirds, but clipped off as a distraction to foliage by some gardeners.HS to Sh. MWD soil.

Joe Pye weed (Eupatorium purpureum) flat-topped clusters of light purple flowers in August, late to start growing in spring; 4' or taller; native to eastern U.S. in wet areas. S to HS. MWD to wet soil.

late season daylily (Hemerocallis varieties) 2 to 3 weeks of bloom from each variety of daylily; late season types bloom July-early August; 1-5'. S to HS, tolerates Sh. MWD soil.

late season Lilium, hybrid lily (Lilium hybrids) erect or pendant trumpet flowers in many colors in late July or early August, whorled foliage on stems from 3-5'. S to HS, tolerates Sh. MWD soil.

Liatris spicata, blazing star - erect wands of purple or mauve, grassy leaves at base of the plant, 18-36", July bloom; native to North American moist meadows, distinct from dry-terrain gayfeather, L. pycnostachya. S to HS. MWD soil.

Lobelia siphilitica, great blue lobelia (Lobelia siphilitica) light blue or white flowers on 18" spikes in July-August; native to moist woods edge and stream-side in Michigan and other parts of North America. HS to S or Sh. MWD to wet soil.

Moonbeam coreopsis (Coreopsis verticillata 'Moonbeam') airy 18" mound, small daisy-like pastel yellow flowers July-August will continue to form into September if deadheaded. S to HS. MWD soil.

Phlox maculata, tall phlox, wild tall phlox (Phlox maculata) fragrant domed clusters of flowers magenta, white, or white with pink eye in July - August; 3-4'; resistant to mildew. HS to S, tolerates Sh. MWD soil.

Phlox paniculata, tall phlox (Phlox paniculata) fragrant domed clusters of flowers pink, violet tones or white in July; 3-4'

Physostegia virginiana 'Alba' and 'Summer Snow', white false dragonshead, white obedient plant - white spikes in July, dark green leaves, 24". S to HS, tolerates Sh. MWD soil.

purple coneflower (Echinacea purpurea) pink daisy-shape flowers on strong stems in July-August; 3-4'; seeds eaten goldfinches & chickadees, butterflies attracted to nectar. S to HS, tolerates Sh. MWD soil.

queen of the prairie (Filipendula rubra venusta) 4' stalks with pink plume flowers in July, large leaves. S to HS, tolerates Sh. MWD to wet soil.

Rudbeckia maxima, giant coneflower - toothed, large oval blue-green leaves clasp stems that rise straight 3-6', bear classic black-eye Susan flowers with tall central cones and drooping petals in late July. S to HS. MWD soil.

Russian sage (Perovskia atriplicifolia) 3-4' gray-green airy plant, light purple flowers in July-early August, entire plant fragrant, semi-evergreen. S, tolerates HS. MWD to dry soil.

sea lavender (Limonium latifolium) basal leaves lay on the ground, leafless flower stalks rise to 24"; mass of light purple flowers in July remain effective throughout summer. S to HS. MWD soil.

Stokes aster (Stokesia laevis) 12" plant with white, violet, pink or blue round-faced, frilled flowers in July-August. S to HS. MWD soil.

summersweet clethera (Clethra alnifolia) - erect shrub, white or pink fragrant flowers in July, good fall color; 5-8' tall x 4-5' wide; variety 'Butterfly' a 3' dwarf; all forms attractive to hummingbirds. HS to S, tolerates Sh. MWD to wet soil.

swamp milkweed (Asclepias incarnata) 4' columnar plant with fragrant rose-pink flowers in July, likes wet soil; not invasive like field milkweed; attracts butterflies and butterfly caterpillars. S to HS. Wet to MWD soil.

trumpet vine (Campsis radicans) vine with orange, red or yellow tubular flowers in July, very showy; self-supporting vine can climb to 75'. S to HS, tolerates Sh. MWD soil.

Veronica longifolia (Veronica longifolia hybrid 'Sunny Border Blue') spikes of blue flowers in July; 18". S to HS. MWD soil.

x Pardancanda norrisii, candylily - sword-shaped foliage, 3' stalks of 1" trumpet like flowers in a wide range of colors (cream, mauve, yellow, orange, bi-colors) July-August, followed by pods filled with shining black seeds in August-September. S to HS. MWD soil.

EARLY AUGUST PEAK BLOOM

Allium senescens glaucum, curly allium
(Allium senescens glaucum) attractive foliage is twisted like sausage curls, does not go dormant as many other alliums do; is less tall and blooms later than the species - lilac flowers in late July-early August; 12". S to HS. MWD soil.

amur maple (Acer ginnala) - multi-stemmed or low-branched tree, good rusty fall color, 25' x 20'; seed pods ("helicopters") are very attractive pink in late July and early August, mistaken for flowers. S to HS. MWD to dry soil.

blue mist caryopteris, blue beard spirea
(Caryopteris x clandonensis) 3-4' round shrub, grey-green leaves, flowers and twigs all fragrant; small blue flowers in showy flat clusters in August. S, tolerates HS. MWD soil.

butterfly bush (Buddleia davidii) 5' woody perennial; slow to start in spring but wonderful in August with fragrant purple, white or lilac conical flower clusters attracting butterflies and hummingbirds. S, tolerates HS. MWD soil.

8 Months of Color

cardinal flower (Lobelia cardinalis) brilliant red flowers on spikes, July-August, columnar plant 3' or taller; avoid red-leaf L. cardinalis hybrids as these are not reliably hardy in Zone 5. For all cardinal flowers, allow seed to set and some seedlings to remain in place, since parent plants often live only two-three years and must be replaced. HS to Sh, S if very moist. MWD to wet soil.

Clara Curtis mum (Chrysanthemum 'Clara Curtis') aggressive pink, daisy-flowered mum; blooms in early August; 15-18". S to HS. MWD soil.

cup plant (Silphium perfoliatum) 6-8' prairie native with yellow August flowers like small sunflowers; large leaves clasp the stem all the way up to the flowers, hold water as if in cups for birds. S. tolerates HS. MWD soil.

dwarf & early goldenrod (Solidago hybrids such as Golden Mosa) yellow plumes in July - August on sturdy plants ranging (by variety) from 18" to 4'. S, tolerates HS. MWD soil.

grape-leaf anemone (Anemone vitifolia) 1-3'; mauve or white flowers in August; foliage with surface and shape like grape leaf; a parent of the summer windflower A. x robustissima, earlier blooming. HS to S. MWD soil.

hardy hibiscus (Hibiscus moscheutos) huge 6-10" floppy-disc flowers in August are red, pink or white; 3' - 5', depending on variety: 'Frisbee' and 'Disco Belle' are 3', species and 'Southern Bell' nearly 5' tall. S . MWD to wet soil.

helianthus x multiflorus, perennial sunflower (Helianthus x multiflorus) large yellow pom-pom flowers on erect 4' plant, blooms July-August. S. MWD soil.

Hypericum shrubby species. S to HS. MWD soil.There are many Hypericum species and varieties available. Dense St. Johnswort (Hypericum densiflorum) and its hybrids tend to bloom later in zone 5 than shrubby St. Johnswort and kalm S. Johnswort - blue green mound 3-4'; large golden flowers in clusters in July-August

ironweed, tall ironweed, Veronia (Vernonia altissima) grey-green foliage; purple flowers in spike-shaped clusters in August on stalks from 3-10' tall; native to Midwest prairie areas. S. MWD to dry soil.

Liatris aspera, rough blazing star, button snakeroot - purple or white flowers clustered in dense buttons, and the buttons dot the upper foot of a stiff 4-6' flower stem; August bloom; native to dry prairies. Sun.

ligularia 'Desdemona', golden groundsel (Ligularia dentata 'Desdemona') daisy-like sulphur-yellow flowers in July-August, large attractive leaves with maroon undersides, 3'. HS to Sh. MWD soil.

Lobelia x speciosa - cardinal flower hybrids such as Gerardii and cardinal flower hybrids; excellent choice for the garden, as tend to be longer-lived than the native parent L. cardinalis; near-fluorescent red, violet, purple or pink flowers in late July-early August; 3' flower stalks above basal foliage. HS to Sh. MWD soil.

Monarda fistulosa, bee balm, horsemint - erect, 3' erect; leaves and flowers fragrant; lilac flowers in July; native to Michigan roadside and woods-edge; likes drier soils than other Monardas. HS, tolerates S or Sh. MWD to dry soil.

northern sea oats (Chasmanthium latifolium) 36" stiffly erect, clump-forming grass Dangling flower/seed heads are flattened as if pressed, become tan and noticeable from a distance in August, persist through winter. S to HS. MWD soil.

patrinia (Patrinia scabiosifolia) 2' chartreuse flowers in dense round-topped clusters in August. S. to HS. MWD soil.

pearly everlasting (Anaphalis margaritacea) grey foliage in dense colony; white button flowers in clusters in August dry in place; 2'. S. MWD to dry soil.

pegee hydrangea (Hydrangea paniculata grandiflora) 5-6' vase-shaped shrub (trained to single-stem tree form increases height to 10-15', white conical clusters of flowers in August age to pink, persist tan through winter. HS to S, tolerates Sh. MWD soil.

8 Months of Color

prairie dock (Silphium terebinthinaceum) huge leaves at ground level and a towering 8-10' leafless flower stalk in August; yellow flowers like mini-sunflowers. Native to moist prairies into at least zone 4. S. MWD to wet soil.

Ratibida laciniata, grey coneflower (Ratibida laciniata) 5-6' columnar plant (though stems may splay out); August blooming; pale yellow daisy-like flowers with drooping petals and gray-green central cones. S. MWD soil, tolerates dry soil.

rose of sharon (Hibiscus syriacus) - columnar or upright spreading shrub; large white, pink or lavender flowers in August; 8-12'. S to HS, tolerates Sh. MWD soil.

scholar tree (Sophora japonica) round-crowned 40-50' deciduous tree, showy white flowers in large conical clusters in August. S to HS. MWD soil.

Sedum rosea, stonecrop- native North American species with dense clusters of rose flowers in early August on 2' stems. S to HS. MWD to dry soil.

sourwood (Oxydendrum arboreum) lustrous dark green leaves turn yellow, red & purple in fall; white fragrant flowers in June; attractive red seed capsules in August are even showier than flowers and persist into fall to contrast with the fall foliage color; 25-30' in height, 20' spread; pyramidal with rounded top and drooping branches. HS to S. MWD soil.

white flowered hosta (Hosta plantaginea) large light green leaves, flower stalks to 3' with large, horizontal white trumpet flowers; sweet scent. HS to Sh. MWD soil.
  • Other late blooming hosta species (representative varieties given): Hosta fortunei ('Hyacinthina', 'Francee', 'Gold Standard'); H. nigrescens; H. plantaginea ('Royal Standard', 'August Moon'); H. tardiflora (Hadspen series such as 'Hadspen Heron', 'Hadspen Blue'); H. lancifolia ('Aureo-variegata'); H. ventricosa; H. ventricosa, 'Sum & Substance', 'Gingko Craig'

LATE AUGUST PEAK BLOOM AND BERRY COLOR

American cranberrybush viburnum, American cranberrybush (Viburnum trilobum) 8-10' rounded shrub; red berries ripen in August, persist through winter. S to HS. MWD soil.

Aralia spinosa, devil's walking stick, Hercules club - small tree, 10-20'; tends to sucker once well established so may be single stemmed tree or shrubby thicket; sharp spines at base of leaf stalks; white plume flower clusters in August very showy; large, divided ferny leaves lend a tropical air; purple-black fruit eaten by birds but fruit stems persist, pinkish and attractive, into fall. S to HS. MWD soil.

astilbe c. pumila, dwarf astilbe (Astilbe chinensis pumila) spikes of mauve flowers in August; low ferny foliage; spreads like a groundcover; 12" plant, 2' in flower. HS to Sh. MWD soil.

blue bush clematis (Clematis davidiana) 3' columnar plant, rather floppy but a good leaner; fragrant clusters of 2" sky blue flowers in August. HS to S or Sh. MWD soil.

boneset, thoroughwort, white Joe Pye (Eupatorium perfoliatum) grey-green foliage is distinctive in that pairs of leaves are united at bases, stem appears to pierce them; white fluff flowers in dense clusters in August; 2-3'; native to moist areas of Midwest. S. MWD to wet soil.

crabapple (Malus hybrids and varieties) fruit ripens red, yellow or orange on crabapples; some varieties hold fruit well into winter. S to HS. MWD soil.

European mountain ash (Sorbus aucuparia) small tree, 25-35'; rounded in outline; clusters of orange to orange-red fruit in August that stay into fall until the birds eat them all; divided leaves give feathery appearance. S to HS. MWD soil.

fall ladies tresses, slender ladies' tresses, green pearl twist (Spiranthes gracilis) late summer and fall blooming native North American orchid; endangered in much of its range, including Michigan; translucent white-green stem and spike of down-facing white flowers blooms in September; 20-30" stem. HS to S or Sh. MWD soil.

fountain grass (Pennisetum alopecuroides) fountain spray of silvery-rose plumes in August, late to begin growth in spring, covers spring bulb plants well; 3'. S. MWD to dry soil.

garlic chives, Chinese chives (Allium tuberosum) garlic-scented foliage low, grassy, gives rise in August to spherical white flower clusters; 18"; spreads rapidly by seed. S to Sh. MWD soil.

Gentian septemfida, crested gentian (Gentian septemfida) dark blue flower in mid to late summer, 4 to 6" tall and 12" wide. S to HS. MWD soil.

Helen's flower (Helenium autumnale) 3-5' columnar plants; rust, and gold tone daisy flowers in August-September. S to HS. MWD soil.

oriental lily, late varieties (Lilium hybrid) trumpet flowers in late Mid to late August (varies by variety), whorled foliage on tall stems; 2-4'. S to HS. MWD soil.

perennial ageratum, blue mist flower (Eupatorium coelestinum) clusters of light blue tufts flower in August, late to start growing in spring; 2'. HS to S, tolerates Sh. MWD soil.

Physostegia virginiana, obedient plant, false dragonshead (Physostegia virginiana) spikes of pink flowers in July-August, lustrous dark green; 3'; blooms later than white flowered form. S to HS, tolerates Sh. MWD soil.

plumbago (Ceratostigma plumbaganoides) groundcover, blue flowers in August, good fall foliage color; 12". HS to S, tolerates Sh. MWD soil.

Sedum (Sedum x 'Vera Jameson') maroon-edged leaves, mounded foliage, flat clusters of rosy flowers in July-August, 12". S to HS. MWD soil.

spearmint (Mentha spicata) aromatic foliage a giveaway on this 30" plant; flowers white, pink or pale lilac in spike clusters in August; aggressive spreader. S to HS. MWD soil.

tall goldenrod (Solidago canadensis, other tall solidago species) columnar plant, plumes of gold flowers in July-August, 2-5'; native North American wildflower. Most species, S to HS; a few species good in Sh. MWD soil.

turtlehead (Chelone obliqua) columnar plant with snapdragon-like pink flowers in August; 3-4'. HS to Sh or S (if wet). MWD soil.

EARLY SEPTEMBER PEAK BLOOM, LEAF AND BERRY COLOR

Aconitum napellus, monkshood - 4' columnar plant; dark blue flowers shaped like the hood of a robe in September; all parts very toxic. S to HS, tolerates Sh. MWD soil.

Aster early species. S to HS, tolerates Sh. MWD soil.
- wood aster or large leaf aster (Aster macrophyllus) 1-4 ft. lavender flowers bloom in late summer; lives at wood edges
- aster, New York aster (Aster novae-belgii) columnar plant if given support, sprawling otherwise, violet range flowers in late August-September; 4' or taller; dwarf varieties exist, mounded 18-36"
- thousand leaf aster (Aster laterifolius) tiny white flowers all along stems, 2'

Eupatorium, late native spp. such as E. rugosum (rough Joe Pye, smokeweed) and E. maculatum (white snakeroot, white sanicle) - purple to white flat-topped flower clusters, 2-3' stems; woods edge. HS to Sh, tolerates S. MWD soil.

gaura (Gaura Lindheimeri) small white flowers dangle from airy stems; 3'; August-September color; short lived perennial, it often acts like a self-sown annual. S to HS. MWD soil.

Helianthus divaricatus, thin leafed sunflower, woods sunflower - 3-4' columnar plant of woods edge; sunflower flowers in August-September. HS to Sh or S. MWD to dry soil.

8 Months of Color

Heptacodium micinoides, seven-son flower - upright shrub or small tree, 15-20' and narrow; fragrant white flowers in clusters, September; attractive pink seed pods in October; no significant fall color; mature bark is white, peeling - very attractive in winter. S to HS. MWD soil.

Japanese anemone, fall windflower (Anemone japonica, syn. Anemone hybrida, Anemone hupehensis) mound of grey-green foliage all summer; tall stems of white or pink poppy-like flowers late August into October; 2-4'. HS to S, tolerates Sh. MWD soil.

Japanese fleece flower, Mexican bamboo; reynoutria fleeceflower (Polygonum cuspidatum) species is extremely aggressive and difficult to eradicate once introduced; better to grow dwarf form 'Compactum' which is slightly less invasive; 2-3' mound of foliage, white flower in August or September followed by bright red seed heads; dwarf is very aggressive groundcover. S to HS, tolerates Sh. MWD soil.

lespedeza, Japanese bush clover (Lespedeza thunbergii) 3-4' erect plant; shrub treated like perennial; rose-purple flowers in September. S to HS. MWD soil.

Miscanthus sinensis 'Purpurescens', purple maiden grass - graceful columnar grass, blades have purple cast, gives appearance of smoky haze; 5'; silvery plumes in late September-October to 6'; good tan feature through winter. S. MWD soil.

showy stonecrop, sedum Autumn Joy (Sedum x telephium 'Autumn Joy') succulent light green foliage, cauliflower-like appearance in July, res, white or pink flowers in August-September; attractive flat clusters of seed pods hold up well throughout winter; 18". S to HS. MWD soil.

silver fleece vine, mile-a-minute vine, silver lace vine (Polygonum aubertii) - fast growing vine to 30', white hanging clusters of flowers in August-September. S to HS, tolerates Sh. MWD soil.

Solidago spathulata , goldenrod - 2', spreading native with light yellow flowers clustered at the tips of the stems in September. S to HS. MWD soil.

Tricyrtis formosana, toadlily - small white, lilac or purple "orchids" held up from erect 2-3' stems in September. HS to Sh. MWD soil.

LATE SEPTEMBER PEAK BLOOM, LEAF AND BERRY COLOR

bluestem goldenrod (Solidago caesia) 3-4' woods-edge plant with yellow flowers in buttons rather than classic goldenrod plumes; blooms in September. HS to Sh. MWD soil.

boltonia (Boltonia asteroides and B. asteroides 'Pink Beauty') 4' column, September bloom, hundreds of tiny white or pink-white flowers; attractive through winter. S to HS. MWD soil.

Brazilian sage(Salvia uliginosa) 18" - 36" plant with attractively lax habit and narrow foliage, September bloom, sky blue flowers unique in the fall garden. S to HS. MWD soil.

burning bush (Euonymus alata) 12-15' shrub, spreads wide at tops like small tree; pinkish red fall color begins in September, continues for extended period; dwarf form (E. alata 'Compacta') 6-8' tall and wide; redder in fall color than species, with pink undertones. S to HS, tolerates Sh. MWD soil.

fall clematis, sweet autumn clematis (Clematis maximowicziana, syn. C. paniculata) large, fast growing vine to 30'; dense clusters of 1" white, starry flowers in late September; fragrant; needs trellis or other sturdy item to twine itself around for support. HS to S. MWD soil.

Indian switch grass, panic grass (Panicum virgatum) 4-5' wispy grass; spreads slowly by runners; attraction is copper haze of tiny seed pods from late September through fall. S. MWD to dry soil.

8 Months of Color

Japanese wax bell (Kirengeshoma palmata) maple-like foliage to 3', an attractive light green mound of neatly arranged leaves all summer, large pale yellow flowers are the wax bells that hang from the tips of stems in October. HS to Sh, tolerates S. MWD soil.

Miscanthus 'Zebrinus', zebra maiden grass (Miscanthus sinensis 'Zebrinus') graceful columnar grass, blades with yellow variegation of horizontal stripes all up leaf blade; 5'; plumes in late September-October to 7'; good tan feature through winter. S. MWD soil.

October daphne (Sedum sieboldii 'October Daphne') blue green leaves edged in maroon, rose flowers in September, 12" mound. HS. MWD soil.

ravenna grass (Erianthus ravennae) clump-forming grass; leaves make a wide fountain 3-4' tall; 12' flowering stalks develop huge point-tipped plumes in late September -October. S. MWD soil.

staghorn sumac (Rhus typhina) classic suckering shrub of roadsides and fields; reddish brown conical seed structure showy at tips of branches in fall and winter; glowing red in September, one of the first shrubs to color. S. MWD soil.

Virginia creeper (Parthenocissus quinquefolia) native deciduous vine; covers the ground and climbs trees to 30' and more; good red early fall color; fast growth; blue late summer berries loved by birds; no significant flower. HS to Sh or S. MWD soil.

Weyrich mum (Dendranthemum Weyrichii, syn. Chrysanthemum Weyrichii) rose-purple single flowers; 12-15" stems; spreads like groundcover. S to HS. MWD soil.

OCTOBER PEAK BLOOM

Aster lateriflolius, thousand leaf aster (Aster lateriflolius) tiny white flowers all along stems, 2'. S to HS, tolerates Sh. MWD soil.

Carmichael monkshood (Aconitum Carmichaelii) 4-5' columnar plant; blue flowers shaped like the hood of a robe in September-October; all parts very toxic. HS to S. MWD soil.

Cimicifuga ramosa, fall fairy candle - flower buds like white pearls effective in September; flowers open to white bottle brushes in late October on 3-4' flower stalks; ferny foliage; purple cast to foliage in variety 'Atropurpurea'. HS to Sh or S. MWD soil.

Colchicum species, fall crocus - 6-8" purple crocus-like flowers in large clusters, emerge without leaf in early October; (leaf grows in spring, dormant by midsummer). S to HS. MWD soil.

Crocus kotschyanus, fall crocus - lilac flowers on naked stems in early October; foliage appears in spring, dies back by early summer. S to HS. MWD soil.

hardy hybrid mum (Chrysanthemum varieties) classic garden mum; normal September bloom time delayed by May-July pinching to remove branch tips; many colors and flowers shapes; 12-24". S to HS. MWD soil.

Helianthus salicifolius, willow leaf sunflower - yellow sunflowers 2" across in October; 4-6'. S to HS. MWD soil.

Miscanthus species. S. MWD soil.
- giant silver grass (Miscanthus floridulus) 8' columnar grass, silvery plumes in October persist through winter
- maiden grass (Miscanthus sinensis varieties) graceful columnar grass, 5', silvery plumes in October, pretty tan through winter

New England aster(Aster novae-anglaie) columnar plant 3-5'; needs staking, or pinching May-July to prevent lodging in fall; white, blue-violet, violet and red-violet flowers delayed until September - October by pinching; dwarf forms available 18-24". S to HS, tolerates Sh. MWD soil.

New York aster (Aster novae-belgii) columnar plant if given support, sprawling otherwise, white, pink, blue or violet range flowers in late August-September; 4' or taller; dwarf varieties exist, mounded 18-36". S to HS, tolerates Sh. MWD soil.

- **nippon mum** (Chrysanthemum nipponicum) mum with white, pink or mauve pom-pom flowers; 1-2' plants. S to HS. MWD soil.
- **sassafras leaf** (Sassafras albidum) native tree. May have gold, red and orange all in one tree in fall. Suckering tree. HS to S MWD soil.
- **Tricyrtis hirta, toadlily** - vase shaped plant; violet speckled flowers at base of upper leaves in October are well-displayed on the upper side of arching stems; 2'. HS to Sh. MWD soil.

NOVEMBER PEAK BLOOM
- **American smoke bush, chittamwood** (Cotinus obovatus) native shrub or small tree, very pretty,. late orange fall color. Truly shows up its European counterpart.
- **callery pear** (Pyrus calleryana) red-orange or purple fall color,one of the latest to color, sometimes at Thanksgiving.
- **paperbark maple** (Acer griseum) deep red-orange fall color,often sudden to develop, usually very late.
- **willows, some crabapples, cranberybush viburnum and silver maples** showing gold later than most trees and shrubs.

INDEX

Acanthus spinosissimus 34
Acer ginnala 24, 39
Acer rubrum 17
Acer saccharinum 16
Acer griseum 45
Achillea filipendulina 34
Achillea millefolium 28
Achillea ptarmica 37
Achillea taygetea 9, 30
Achillea The Pearl 11, 37
aconite 16
Aconitum Carmichaelii 44
Aconitum napellus 13, 42
Actaea pachypoda 24
Actaea rubra 29
Adenophora liliifolia 35
Adonis 5, 17
Adonis amurensis 17
Aesculus hippocastanum 22
Aesculus parviflora 30
Aesculus x carnea23
ajuga6, 18
Ajuga repens 18
Alcea rosea 38
Alchemilla alpina 27
Alchemilla mollis 27
Alchemilla vulgaris 27
Allium aflatunense 24
Allium caeruleum 24
Allium Christophii 24
Allium giganteum 26
Allium globosum 24
Allium moly 24
Allium neopolitanum 24
Allium ostrowskianum 24
Allium pulchellum 24
Allium senescens 11, 37
Allium senescens glacum 12, 39
Allium species 8, 24
Allium tuberosum 42
alpine aster 7, 20
alpine currant 7, 20
alternate leaf dogwood 8, 24

Amelanchier canadensis 20
Amelanchier stolonifera 20
American cranberrybush
viburnum 7, 12, 21, 41
American cranberrybush 21, 41
American elderberry 8, 24
American smokebush 45
American smokebush leaf 14
American smoke tree 37
American vetch 28
American witchhazel 14
Amsonia tabernaemontana 24
Amur adonis 17
Amur honeysuckle 7, 21
amur maple 8, 12, 13, 24, 39
Anacylus 30
Anacyclus depressus 9, 30
Anaphalis margaritacea 40
Anemone blanda 6, 18
Anemone canadensis 21
Anemone hupehensis 43
Anemone hybrida 43
Anemone japonica 43
Anemone pulsatilla 18
Anemone sylvestris 6, 18
Anemone vitifolia 40
Anemone x robustissima 11, 37
angelica 8, 24
Angelica archangelica 24
Antennaria dioica 28
Anthemis tinctoria 32
apricot 6, 18
Aquilegia 21
Arabis blepharophylla 20
Arabis caucasica 20
Arabis species 20
Aralia spinosa 12, 41
Arenaria verna caespitosa 27
Aristolochia durior 21
Armeria maritima 23
arrowwood viburnum 8, 14, 24
Aruncus aethusifolius 35
Aruncus dioicus 32
Asclepias incarnata 39

Asclepias tuberosa 35
ash leaf 14
aspen leaf 14
Aster alpinus 20
Aster early species 13, 42
Aster laterifolius 14, 42, 44
Aster macrophyllus 42
Aster novae-anglaie 44
Aster novae-belgii 42, 44
Astilbe chinensis 37
Astilbe chinensis pumila 12, 41
Astilbe simplicifolia 10, 34
Astilbe taquetii 11, 37
Astilbe x arendsii 31, 35
Astrantia 9, 30
Astrantia carniolica 30
Astrantia major 30
Astrantia major rubra 30
Aubrieta deltoidea 5, 17
Aurinia saxatilis 20
Autumn Joy 43
autumn olive 8, 24
baby's breath 10, 34
bald cypress leaf 14
balloon flower 11, 37
Baptisia australis 26
basswood 33
bear's breeches 10, 34
beardtongue 33
beauty bush 8, 25
bee balm 10, 34, 40
Belamcanda chinensis 37
bellflower 8, 10, 25, 36
bergenia 6, 18
Bergenia cordifolia 18
Bethlehem sage 18
biennial blackeye Susan 9, 30
bigleaf forget-me-not 18
bigleaf hydrangea 37
bigroot perennial geranium 22
birdsfoot trefoil 9, 30
bishop's hat 19
bistort 28
black locust 8, 14, 25
blackberry lily 11, 37
blackeye Susan 30, 38
black gum leaf 14
blanket flower 32

blazing star 38, 40
bleeding heart 6, 18
blood-red geranium 23
blue beard spirea 39
bluebells of Scotland 31
blue bush clematis 12, 41
blue clips 31
blue fescue 8, 25
blue flax 9, 30
blue fringed bleeding heart 9, 30
blue globe thistle 11, 37
blue linaria 10, 34
blue mist caryopteris 12, 39
blue mist flower 42
blue oat grass 8, 25
blue-eyed grass 8, 25
blue hydrangea 11, 37
bluestem goldenrod 13, 43
blue toadflax 34
blue wild snapdragon 34
boltonia 13, 43
Boltonia asteroides 43
boneset 12, 41
border jewel 33
Boston ivy leaf 14
bottlebrush buckeye 9, 30
Bouncing Bet 11, 37
Bowles golden grass 8, 25
boys and girls 18
Brazilian sage 13, 43
bridal wreath spirea 7, 21
brodiaea laxa 35
Bumalda spirea leaf 14
Brunnera macrophylla 6, 18
Buddleia davidii 39
bull thistle 9, 30
Bupthalmum salicifolium 10, 34
Burkwood viburnum 7, 21
burnet 36
burning bush 13, 43
butterfly bush 12, 39
butterfly weed 10, 35
buttonbush 10, 35
calamint 10, 35
Calamintha Nepeta 35
callery pear 6, 14, 18, 45
California hyacinth 10, 35

Caltha palustris 18
Calycanthus floridus 7, 21
camas 21
Camassia cusickii 7, 21
Campanula carpatica 31
Campanula glomerata 25
Campanula poscharskyana 36
Campanula rotundifolia 31
Campsis radicans 39
Canada anemone 7, 21
candylily 39
candytuft 20
Caragana arborescens 23
Caragana arborescens 'Pendula' 23
cardinal flower 12, 40
cardinal flower hybrids 40
Carex stricta 25
Carmichael monkshood 14, 44
Carolina allspice 21
Carolina lupine 9, 30
Carolina silverbell 7, 21
Carpathian harebell 9, 31
Caryopteris x clandonensis 39
Castanea mollissima 35
Catalpa speciosa 33
Catananche caerulea 35
catmint 7, 21
celandine poppy 6, 19
Centaurea dealbata 8, 25
Centaurea montana 22
Centranthus ruber 35
Cephalanthus occidentalis 35
Cerastium tomentosum 29
Ceratostigma plumbaganoides 42
Cercis canadensis 20
Chaenomeles japonica 20
Chaenomeles speciosa 20
Chasmanthium latifolium 40
cheddar pinks 8, 25
Chelone obliqua 42
chestnut 10, 35
child of two worlds 32
Chinese chestnut 35
Chinese chives 42
Chinese lantern 10, 35
chittamwood 37, 45

Chrysanthemum 'Clara Curtis' 40
Chrysanthemum coccineum 28
Chrysanthemum leucanthemum 22
Chrysanthemum nipponicum 45
Chrysanthemum parthenium 31
Chrysanthemum varieties 44
Chrysanthemum Weyrichii 44
Chrysanthemum x superbum 36
Cimicifuga racemosa 11, 37
Cimicifuga ramosa 14, 44
Cirsium vulgare 30
Clara Curtis mum 12, 40
Claytonia virginica 18
clematis 27
Clematis davidiana 41
Clematis hybrid 27
Clematis maximowicziana 43
Clematis paniculata 43
Clematis recta 9, 31
Clematis viticella 9, 31
Clethra alnifolia 39
climbing hydrangea 8, 25
clove currant 6, 19
clustered bellflower 8, 25
Colchicum species 14, 44
columbine 7, 21
columbine meadow rue 27
common harebell 9, 31
common hyacinth 17
common ladies' tresses 26
common lilac 7
common locust 25
common thyme 8, 25
common privet 8, 25
coneflower 36, 39, 41
Cotinus obovata
Cotinus obovatus 45
contorted hazel 4, 16
Convallaria majalis 22
coral bell 35
coral bells 8, 25
Coreopsis auriculata 28
Coreopsis lanceolata 32
Coreopsis rosea 10, 35
Coreopsis verticillata 34, 38
cornelian cherry 4, 16
Cornus alba sibirica 23
Cornus alternifolia 24

Cornus florida 22
Cornus kousa 27
Cornus mas 16
Cornus racemosa 32
Coronilla varia 31
Corydalis flexuosa 30
Corydalis lutea 9, 31
Corylus avellana 16
Cotinus coggygria 37
Cotinus obovata 37
Cotoneaster 8, 25
Cotoneaster adpressus 25
Cotoneaster apiculatus 25
Cotoneaster divaricatus 25
cowslip 18
crabapple 7, 12, 14, 21, 41, 45
crambe 25
Crambe cordifolia 8, 25
Crambe maritima 8, 26
cranberry cotoneaster 25
cranberybush viburnum 45
Crataegus crusgalli 27
Crataegus laevigata 27
Crataegus phaenopyrum 34
Crataegus x Lavallei 27
creeping baby's breath 8, 26
creeping cotoneaster 25
creeping forget-me-not 8, 26
creeping phlox 6, 19
creeping soapwort 7, 21
creeping St. Johnswort 35
creeping veronica 24
crested gentian 42
crocosmia 11, 38
Crocosmia hybrid 'Lucifer' 38
Crocus chrysanthus 16
crocus Dutch hybrids 16
Crocus kotschyanus 14, 44
Crocus minimus 16
crown vetch 9, 31
culinary sage 7, 21
culver's root 11, 38
cup plant 12, 40
Cupid's dart 10, 35
curly allium 37, 39
cushion spurge 6, 19
cut-leaf stephanandra 8, 26
daffodil 6, 17, 19

Dalmation geranium 32
dame's rocket 7, 21
dark-eyed perennial geranium 22
daylily 9, 10, 11, 27, 31
day primrose 37
deciduous azalea 22
delphinium 9, 31
Delphinium elatum 31
Dendranthemum Weyrichii 44
Dentaria diphylla 20
Deutzia gracilis 23
devil's walking stick 41
Dianthus alpinus 26
Dianthus barbatus 29
Dianthus gratianopolitanus 25
Dianthus plumarius 26
Dianthus species 7, 8, 21, 26
Dianthus x alwoodii 26
Dicentra cucullaria 17
Dicentra eximia 19
Dicentra spectabilis 18
Dictamnus purpureus 22
Digitalis ambigua 31
Digitalis lutea 31
Digitalis mertonensis 31
Digitalis purpureus 26
Digitalis species 9, 31
dogtooth violet 20
doll's eyes 24
Doronicum caucasicum 19
doublefile viburnum 8, 14, 26
double geranium 22
Draba 5, 17
Draba Haynaldii 17
dropwort 8, 26
Dutch crocus 4, 16
Dutch hyacinth 5, 17
Dutchman's breeches 5, 17
Dutchman's pipe vine 7, 21
dwarf astilbe 41
dwarf bearded iris 7, 21
dwarf bulb iris 16
dwarf Fothergilla 5, 14, 17
dwarf goatsbeard 9, 35
dwarf goldenrod 12, 40
dwarf lilac 26, 27

dwarf lilac Miss Kim 8, 26
dwarf pincushion 33
dwarf potentilla 23
dwarf spirea 9, 31
early astilbe hybrids 9, 10, 31, 35
early daffodils 5, 17
early goldenrod 12, 40
early ladies tresses 8, 26
early Lilium species 9, 31
early/repeating daylily 9
early rhododendron 20
Echinacea pallida 36
Echinacea purpurea 39
Echinops exaltatus 37
edelweiss 11, 38
Elaeagnus umbellata 24
English thyme 25
Epilobium angustifolium 31
Epimedium species 6, 19
Eranthis hyemalis 16
Eremurus himalaicus 26
Erianthus ravennae 44
Eryngium planum 36
Erythronium canadensis 20
Euonymus alata 43
Euonymus fortunei radicans 34
Eupatorium species, late 13, 42
Eupatorium coelestinum 42
Eupatorium maculatum 42
Eupatorium perfoliatum 41
Eupatorium purpureum 38
Eupatorium rugosum 42
Euphorbia griffithii 7, 22
Euphorbia myrsinites 19
Euphorbia polychroma 19
European cranberry viburnum 7, 22
European mountain ash 8, 12, 26, 41
European woods anemone 18
evening-flowered primrose 33
everlasting 28
Exbury azalea 7, 22
fairy candle 37
fall clematis 13, 43
fall crocus 44
fall fairy candle 44
fall ladies tresses 12, 41

fall windflower 43
false dragonshead 42
false indigo 8, 26
false rock cress 17
false sunflower 35
fernleaf yarrow 34
Festuca ovina glauca 25
feverfew 9, 31
field daisy 22
Filipendula rubra venusta 39
Filipendula hexapetala 26
Filipendula ulmaria 36
Filipendula vulgaris 26
flowering pear 18
fireglow euphorbia 22
firethorn 8, 26
fireweed 9, 31
flowering dogwood 7, 13, 22
foamflower 6, 19
forget-me-not 22
forsythia 5, 17, 19
Forsythia suspensa 17
Forsythia x intermedia 17
Fothergilla gardenii 17
fountain grass 12, 42
foxglove 8, 26, 31
foxtail lily 8, 26
Fragaria virginiana 29
fringed bleeding heart 6, 19
Gaillardia 9, 32
Gaillardia x grandiflora 32
Galium odoratum 20
gardener's garters 36
garden heliotrope 30
garden hyacinth 17
garlic chives 12, 42
gas plant 7, 22
gaura 13, 42
Gaura Lindheimeri 42
Gentian septemfida 12, 42
geranium Ballerina 23
Geranium cinereum 23
Geranium dalmaticum 9, 32
Geranium endressi 22
Geranium himalayense 22
Geranium 'Johnson's Blue' 23
Geranium macrorrhizum 22
Geranium maculatum 22

Geranium psilostemon 22
Geranium sanguineum 23
German statice 11, 38
geum 7, 22
Geum coccinea 22
Geum triflorum 28
giant allium 8, 26
giant coneflower 39
giant flowering onion 26
gingko leaf 14
Gladiolus byzantinus 28
Gleditsia triacanthos 27
globeflower 23
Gnaphalium leontopodium 38
goatsbeard 9, 32
golden bleeding heart 31
golden chain tree 8, 27
golden groundsel 40
golden Marguerite 9, 32
golden rain tree 11, 38
goldenrod 43
Goldsturm rudbeckia 11, 38
Goniolimon tataricum 38
gooseneck 11, 38
grape hyacinth 6, 19
grape-leaf anemone 12, 40
grape vine leaf 14
grass 8, 12, 25, 36, 40, 42, 43, 44
graystem dogwood 9, 13, 32
great blue lobelia 38
Grecian windflower 18
green pearl twist 41
Greigii tulips 5, 17
grey coneflower 41
Gypsophila paniculata 34
Gypsophila repens 26
Halesia carolina 21
Hamamelis mollis hybrids 16
Hamamelis vernalis hybrids 16
hard maple 16
hardy catalpa 33
hardy hibiscus 12, 40
hardy hybrid mum 14, 44
harebell 9, 31
Harry Lauder's walking stick 16
hawkweed 30
hawthorn 8, 14, 27
Heckrott honeysuckle 9, 32

Helen's flower 12, 42
Helenium autumnale 42
Helianthus divaricatus 13, 42
Helianthus salicifolius 14, 44
Helianthus x multiflorus 12, 40
Helictotrichon sempervirens 25
Heliopsis scabra 10, 35
heliotrope 30
Helleborus x orientalis 16
Hemerocallis 31, 36, 38
Hemerocallis lilioasphodelus 27
Hemerocallis Stella D'oro 31
hepatica 5, 17
Hepatica acutiloba 17
Heptacodium micinoides 13, 43
Hercules club 41
Hesperis matronalis 21
Heuchera sanguinea 25
Heuchera x brizoides 10, 35
heucherella 7, 22
Heucherella tiarelloides 22
hickory leaf 14
Hibiscus moscheutos 40
Hibiscus syriacus 41
Hieracium species 30
Himalayan fleeceflower 33
hoary vervain 11, 38
hollyhock 11, 38
hollyhock mallow 10, 35
honesty 19
honey locust 8, 13, 27
honeysuckle 7, 9, 21, 32
horned violet 17
horsechestnut 7, 22
horsemint 40
hosta 9, 11, 32, 38, 41
Hosta decorata 32, 38
Hosta fortunei 41
Hosta hypoleuca 32, 38
Hosta lancifolia 41
Hosta nakaiana32, 38
Hosta nigrescens 41
Hosta plantaginea 41
Hosta sieboldiana 32, 38
Hosta tardiana 32, 38
Hosta tardiflora 41
Hosta undulata 32

Hosta ventricosa 41
Hosta venusta 32
hundreds and thousands 18
husker red penstemon 33
Hyacinthus orientalis 17
hybrid lily 36, 38
Hydrangea anomala petiolaris 25
Hydrangea arborescens 37
Hydrangea macrophylla 37
Hydrangea paniculata grandiflora 40
Hydrangea quercifolia 36
Hypericum calycinum 10, 35
Hypericum densiflorum 35
Hypericum kalmianum 35
Hypericum prolificum 35
Hypericum shrubby species 10, 12, 35, 40
Iberis sempervirens 20
Iceland poppy 8, 27
Ilex verticillata 34
Indian switch grass 13, 43
Indian quamash 21
Inula ensifolia 33
iris, bearded types 8, 27
Iris germanica 21, 27
Iris Kaempferi 32
Iris pallida 9, 32
Iris pallida variegata 32
Iris pseudacorus 30
Iris pseudacorus variegata 30
Iris reticulata 4, 16
Iris sibirica 29
Irish moss 8, 27
ironweed 12, 40
Itea virginica 34
Jacob's Ladder 8, 27
Japanese andromeda 5, 17
Japanese anemone 13, 43
Japanese bush clover 43
Japanese fleece flower 13, 43
Japanese iris 9, 32
Japanese kerria 8, 27
Japanese stewartia 37
Japanese tree lilac 29
Japanese wax bell 13, 44
Jasione perennis 9, 32

Joe Pye weed 11, 38
Johnny smoke 28
juneberry 20
Jupiter's beard 10, 35
kalm St. Johnswort 35
Kaufmaniana tulips 5, 18
Kerria japonica 27
kingcup 18
Kirengeshoma palmata 44
Knautia macedonica 9, 32
Kniphofia uvaria 36
Koelreuteria paniculata 38
Kolkwitzia amabilis 25
Korean lilac 8, 27
koreanspice viburnum 6, 19
kousa dogwood 8, 27
Laburnum x watererii 27
lacecap hydrangea 37
ladies' tobacco 28
ladies' tresses 26, 41
lady bells 10, 35
lady's mantle 8, 27
lamb's ears 9, 32
lanceleaf coreopsis 9, 32
larch leaf 14
large-flowered clematis 8, 27
large-flowered comfrey 6, 19
large-flowered trillium 6, 19
large leaf aster 42
late clematis 31
late tulip 7, 22
late season daylily 11, 38
lateseason Lilium 11, 38
Lathyrus latifolius 33
Lathyrus vernus 24
Lavandula angustifolia 35
lavender 10, 35
lavender mist meadow rue 27
lemon lily 8, 27
lemon thyme 9, 32
Lenten rose 4, 16
Leontopodium alpinum 38
leopardsbane 6, 19
lespedeza 43
Lespedeza thunbergii 13, 43
Leucanthemum superbum 22, 36
Leucojum Gravetye 20
Liatris aspera 12, 40

Liatris pycnostachya 38
Liatris spicata 11, 38
Ligularia dentata 'Desdemona' 12, 40
Ligularia stenocephala 'The Rocket' 36
Ligustrum x Golden Vicary 25
lilac 21
lilac locust 29
lilac sage 33
Lilium candidum 36
Lilium hybrids 31, 36, 38, 42
Lilium philadelphicum 34
Lilium species 10
lily of the valley 7, 22
Limonium latifolium 39
Limonium tataricum 38
Linaria purpurea 34
linden 9, 14, 32
Linum perenne 30
Liriodendron tulipifera 30
littleleaf linden 32
Lobelia cardinalis 40
Lobelia siphilitica 11, 38
Lobelia x speciosa 12, 40
locust 25, 27, 29
Lonicera tatarica 21
Lonicera x Heckrottii 32
loosestrife 33, 36, 38
Lotus corniculatus 30
low-grow sumac leaf 14
Lunaria annua 19
lungwort 18
lupine 8, 27
Lupinus hybrids 27
Lychnis chalcedonica 36
Lychnis coronaria 33
Lysimachia ciliata 10, 36
Lysimachia clethroides 38
Lysimachia ephemerum 10, 36
Lysimachia punctata 9, 33
madonna lily 10, 36
Magnolia stellata 18
Magnolia virginiana 29
Magnolia x soulangiana 20
maiden grass 43, 44
Maltese cross 10, 36
Malus hybrids 21
Malus x sargentii 23
Malva Alcea 35

marsh marigold 5, 18
masterwort 30
May-blob 18
meadow-bright 18
meadow rue 8, 27
Mentha spicata 42
merry bells 6, 19
Mertensia virginica 24
Mexican bamboo 43
Michigan holly 34
mid-season daylily 10, 36
mid-season Lilium 36
mid-season tulip 6, 19
mile-a-minute vine 43
Milfoil yarrow 8, 28
milkweed 39
mini hollyhock 36
mini iris 16
Miscanthus sinensis 'Purpurescens' 13, 43
Miscanthus sinensis 'Zebrinus' 13, 44
Miscanthus species 14, 44
Missouri primrose 9, 33
mock orange 8, 28
Monarda didyma 34
Monarda fistulosa 12, 40
money plant 6, 19
monkshood 42, 44
Moonbeam coreopsis 11, 34, 38
mophead hydrangea 37
mother of thyme 25
Mountain Bluet 7, 22
mountain phlox 28
mouse-ear coreopsis 8, 28
mouse-ear forget-me-not 7, 22
mullein 24, 34
multi-flowered tulip 17
multiflora rose 33
mum 44
Muscari armeniacum 19
Myosotis biennis 22
Myosotis scorpioides 26
myrtle 6, 19
myrtle euphorbia 6, 19
nannyberry viburnum 7, 22
Narcissus hybrid 17, 19

Narcissus species 19
Nectaroscordum siculum 8, 28
Nepeta Mussinii 21
New England aster 14, 44
New York aster 14, 42, 44
ninebark 8, 28
nippon mum 14, 45
nodding ladies tresses 26
northern catalpa 9, 33
northern sea oats 12, 40
Norway maple leaf 14
oakleaf hydrangea 10, 36
obedient plant 39, 42
October daphne 13, 44
Oenethera caespitosa 9, 33
Oenethera missouriensis 33
Oenethera speciosa 9, 33
Oenethera speciosa/rosea 33
Oenethera tetragona 37
old man's whiskers 28
oriental lily 12, 31, 36, 42
oriental poppy 8, 28
ornamental cherry 5, 18
ornamental locust 29
ornamental rhubarb 8, 28
Ornithogalum nutans 23
oxeye 34
oxeye daisy 7, 22
Oxydendrum arboreum 41
Pieris floribunda hybrid 17
Paeonia lactiflora 28
Pagoda dogwood 24
painted daisy 8, 28
pale purple coneflower 10, 36
palibin lilac 27
panic grass 43
Panicum virgatum 43
Papaver atlanticum 23
Papaver nudicaule 27
Papaver orientale 28
paperbark maple 14, 45
Pardancanda norrisii 11, 39
Parthenocissus quinquefolia 44
pasque flower 5, 18
pasture rose 33
patrinia 12, 40

Patrinia scabiosifolia 40
pea vetch 8, 28
pearly everlasting 12, 40
peegee hydrangea 12, 40
Pennisetum alopecuroides 42
Penstemon digitalis 33
Penstemon hirsutus 33
Penstemon nitidus 33
Penstemon pinifolius 33
Penstemon species 9, 33
pepperroot 20
peony 8, 28
perennial ageratum 12, 42
perennial alyssum 6, 20
perennial candytuft 6, 20
perennial blackeye Susan 38
perennial foxglove 31
perennial geranium 7, 22
perennial gladiola 8, 28
perennial salvia 29
perennial sunflower 40
perennial sweet pea 9, 33
perennial yellow foxglove 31
Perovskia atriplicifolia 39
Persian cornflower 25
Phalaris arundinacea 'Picta' 36
pheasant's eye 17
Philadelphus x virginicus 28
Phlomis russeliana 10, 36
Phlox maculata 11, 38
Phlox ovata 8, 28
Phlox paniculata 11, 38
Phlox stolonifera 20
Phlox subulata 19
Physalis Alkekengi 35
Physocarpus opulifolius 28
Physostegia virginiana 11, 12, 39, 42
Physostegia, white 11
Pieris japonica 17
pincushion flower 9, 33
pineapple shrub 21
pink hydrangea 11, 37
pink perennial geranium 22
pink primrose 33
pink threadleaf coreopsis 35
PJM rhododendron 6, 20
Platycodon grandiflorus 37

plumbago 12, 42
poison ivy leaf 14
poker plant 36
polecat weed 16
Polemonium caeruleum 27
Polygonatum biflorum 29
Polygonatum odoratum variegatum 29
Polygonum affine 9, 33
Polygonum aubertii 43
Polygonum Bistorta 8, 28
Polygonum cuspidatum 43
potentilla 7, 8, 23, 28
Potentilla alba 23
Potentilla atrosanguinea 9, 33
Potentilla fruticosa 28
Potentilla nepalensis 23
Potentilla verna nana 23
prairie dock 12, 41
prairie smoke 8, 28
pink primrose 33
primrose 18
Primula x polyantha 5, 18
privet 25
Prunella vulgaris 29
Prunella vulgaris laciniata 29
Prunus armeniaca 18
Prunus sargenti 18
Prunus species 18
Prunus x yedoensis 18
Pulmonaria saccharata 5, 18
Pulsatilla vulgaris 18
purple coneflower 11, 39
purple maiden grass 43
purple meadow sage 33
purple mullein 24
purple vetch 28
puschkinia 5, 17
Puschkinia scillioides 17
pussy's toes 8, 28
Pyracantha coccinea 26
Pyrus calleryana 18, 45
queen of the meadow 10, 36
queen of the prairie 11, 39
quince 6, 20
Ranunculus acris 23
Ratibida laciniata 12, 41
ravenna grass 13, 44

red baneberry 8, 29
red field poppy 7, 23
red horsechestnut 7, 23
red hot poker 10, 36
red maple 5, 14, 17
redbud 6, 20
redtwig dogwood 7, 23
reynoutria fleeceflower 43
Rheum palmatum 28
Rhododendron 20
Rhododendron hybrids 20, 22
rhubarb 28
Rhus typhina 44
ribbon grass 10, 36
Ribes alpinum 20
Ribes odoratum 19
river maple 16
Robinia pseudoacacia 25
Robinia x ambigua 8, 29
rock cress 6, 20
Rocket ligularia 10, 36
rock maple 16
rodgersia 29
Rodgersia species 8, 29
Rosa multiflora 9, 33
rose 33
rose allium 24
rose masterwort 30
rose of sharon 12, 41
Rudbeckia fulgida 30
Rudbeckia fulgida 'Goldsturm' 38
Rudbeckia maxima 11, 39
running serviceberry 20
Russian sage 11, 39
sage 18, 21, 29, 33, 39, 43
Salvia azurea 29
Salvia grandiflora 29
Salvia officinalis 21
Salvia species 8, 29
Salvia x superba 8, 29
Salvia uliginosa 43
Salvia verticillata 9, 33
Sambucus canadensis 24
Sanguisorba obtusa 10, 36
Saponaria ocymoide 21
Saponaria officinalis 37
Sargent crabapple 7, 23

Sassafras leaf 14, 45
Sassafras albidum 45
saucer magnolia 6, 20
Scabiosa 'Butterfly blue' 9, 33
Scabiosa caucasica 33
Scabiosa columbaria 33
scarlet campion 9, 33
scarlet cinquefoil 33
scarlet maple 17
scholar tree 12, 41
Scilla sibirica 16
sea crambe 26
sea holly 10, 36
sea lavender 11, 39
sea pinks 7, 23
sedum 8, 29, 42
Sedum acre 29
sedum Autumn Joy 43
Sedum kamschaticum 29
sedum rosea 12, 41
Sedum sieboldii 'October Daphne' 44
Sedum x 'Vera Jameson' 12, 42
Sedum x telephium 43
self-heal 8, 29
Serbian bellflower 10, 36
serviceberry 6, 14, 20
seven-son flower 43
shad 20
shadblow 20
sharp-leafed liverwort 17
Shasta daisy 10, 36
sheepberry 22
sheep's bit 32
sheep's fescue 25
showy mullein 34
showy stonecrop 13, 43
shrubby St. Johnswort 35
Siberian iris 8, 29
Siberian pea shrub/tree 7, 23
Sidalcea 10, 36
Sidalcea malviflora 36
Silphium perfoliatum 40
Silphium terebinthinaceum 41
silverbell 21
silver fleece vine 13, 43
silver lace vine 43

silver maple 4, 14, 16, 45
Sisyrinchium angustifolium 25
skunk cabbage 4, 16
slender deutzia 7, 23
slender ladies' tresses 41
smoke bush 37
smoke tree 10, 37
snakeweed 28
snow crocus 4, 16
snow in summer 8, 29
snowball hydrangea 10, 37
snowball viburnum 7, 23
snowdrops 4, 16
snowmound spirea 23
soapwort 21
soft maple 16, 17
Solidago caesia 43
Solidago canadensis 42
Solidago hybrids 40
Solidago spathulata 13, 43
Solomon's seal 8, 29
Sophora japonica 41
Sorbaria sorbifolia 37
Sorbus aucuparia 26, 41
sourwood 12, 41
spearmint 12, 42
spiderwort 8, 29
spike speedwell 34
spiny bear's breeches 34
Spiraea japonica 31
Spiraea prunifolia 21
Spiraea vanhouttei 23
Spiraea x bumalda 31
Spiranthes cernuum 26
Spiranthes gracilis 41
spotted loosestrife 33
spring beauty 5, 18
spring witchhazel 4, 16
spreading cotoneaster 25
squill 4, 16
St. Johnswort 35, 40
Stachys lanata 32
staghorn sumac 13, 44
star magnolia 5, 18
star of Bethlehem 7, 23
Stephanandra incisa 26
Stewartia pseudocamellia 10, 14, 37

Stokes aster 11, 39
Stokesia laevis 39
stonecrop 41
strawberry 8, 29
strawberry shrub 21
strawberry tomato 35
Stylophorum diphyllum 19
sugar maple 4, 13, 16
summer snowflake 6, 20
summersweet clethra 11, 14, 39
sundrops primrose 10, 37
sunflower 35, 40, 42, 44
sunny twinkles 24
swamp buttercup 7, 23
swamp maple 17
swamp milkweed 11, 39
sweet autumn clematis 43
sweet bay magnolia 8, 29
sweet flag 30
sweet gum leaf 14
sweet pea 24, 33
sweet rocket 21
sweetshrub 21
sweet William 8, 29
sweet woodruff 6, 20
swordleaf inula 9, 33
Symphytum grandiflorum 19
Symplocarpus foetidus 16
Syringa meyeri 27
Syringa patula 26
Syringa reticulata 29
Syringa vulgaris 21
tall goldenrod 12, 42
tall ironweed 40
tall phlox 38
tarda tulip 5, 17
Tatarian honeysuckle 21
thalictrum 27
Thalictrum aquilegifolium 27
Thalictrum rochebrunianum 27
Thermopsis caroliniana 30
thin leafed sunflower 42
thoroughwort 41
thousand leaf aster 42, 44
thousand-leaf yarrow 28
threadleaf coreopsis 9, 34
thyme 25, 32

Thymus x citriodorus 32
Thymus serpyllum 25
Tiarella cordifolia 19
Tilia americana 33
Tilia cordata 32
toadflax 34
toadlily 43, 45
toothwort 6, 20
torch plant 36
Trollius 7, 23
Tradescantia virginiana 29
tree lilac 8, 29
Tricyrtis formosana 13, 43
Tricyrtis hirta 14, 45
trillium 19
Trillium grandiflorum 19
Tritelia laxa 35
Trollius europaeus 7, 23
trout lily 6, 20
trumpet vine 11, 39
Tulipa 22
Tulipa daysystemon 17
Tulipa Greigii 17
Tulipa hybrids 19
Tulipa Kaufmaniana 18
Tulipa turkestanica 5, 17
tulip tree 30
tulip poplar 8, 14, 30
turtlehead 12, 42
twisted filbert 16
Ural false spirea 10, 37
Uvularia grandiflora 19
valerian 30
Valeriana officinalis 8, 30
Vanhoutte spirea 7, 23
varied-leaf harebell 31
variegated Solomon's seal 29
Venetian sumac 37
Verbascum 24, 34
Verbascum Cotswold hybrids 9, 34
Verbascum phoeniceum 7, 24
Verbena hastata 38
vernal sweet pea 7, 24
Veronia 40
Vernonia altissima 40
Veronica incana 34
Veronica longifolia 11, 39

Veronica prostrata 7, 24
veronica species 9, 34
Veronica spicata 34
Veronica subsessilis 34
Veronicastrum virginicum 38
Viburnum carlesii 19
Viburnum dentatum 24
Viburnum lentago 22
Viburnum opulus 22, 23
Viburnum plicatum tomentosum 26
Viburnum trilobum 21, 41
Viburnum x Burkwoodii 21
Vicia americana 28
Vinca minor 19
vine euonymus 9, 34
vine honeysuckle 32
Viola cornuta 17
Viola hybrids 16
viola, pansy 4, 16
violet pea tree 29
Virginia bluebells 7, 24
Virginia creeper 13, 44
Virginia sweetspire 9, 34
Virgin's bower 27
Washington hawthorn 9, 34
wax bells 44
weeping cherry 18
weeping pea 23
weeping yoshino cherry 18
weigela 8, 30
Weigela florida 30
Weyrich mum 13, 45
white baneberry 7, 24
white clips bellfower 31
white false dragonshead 39
white flowered hosta 12, 41
white flowering onion 24
white Joe Pye 41
white locust 25
white maple 16
white oak leaf 14
white obedient plant 39
wickup 31
wild perennial geranium 22
wild tall phlox 38
wild violet 5, 17

willow leaf sunflower 44
willows 45
willow amsonia 7, 24
willow leaf sunflower 25
windflower 18, 37, 43
winter aconite 4, 16
winterberry 9, 34
winter cherry 35
wisteria 8, 30
Wisteria chinensis 30
witchhazel 4, 14, 16, 45
wood anemone 18
wood aster 42
wood lily 9, 34
woodland phlox 6, 20
woods sunflower 42
yarrow 28, 30, 34
yellow flag iris 8, 30
yellow foxglove 31
yellow fumitory 31
yellow hawkweed 8, 30
yellow locust 25
yellow loosestrife 33
yellow sweet flag 30
yellow yarrow 9, 34
yellowwood leaf 14
yucca 10, 37
Yucca filamentosa 37
zebra iris 32
zebra maiden grass 44